a.99

OPERATIONS MANAGEMENT

An analytical and evaluative approach to business studies

To be

OPERATIONS MANAGEMENT

An analytical and evaluative approach to business studies

Simon Harrison, Ian Swift, Andrew Gillespie

Hodder & Stoughton

A MEMBER OF THE HODDER HEADLINE GROUP

Orders: please contact Bookpoint Ltd, 78 Milton Park, Abingdon, Oxon OX14 4TD. Telephone: (44) 01235 827720, Fax: (44) 01235 400454. Lines are open from 9.00–6.00, Monday to Saturday, with a 24 hour message answering service. Email address: orders@bookpoint.co.uk

British Library Cataloguing in Publication Data
A catalogue record for this title is available from The British Library

ISBN 0 340 779667

First published 2000
Impression number   10 9 8 7 6 5 4 3 2 1
Year   2005 2004 2003 2002 2001 2000

Cover illustration by Jon H. Hamilton
Typeset by Fakenham Photosetting Ltd, Fakenham, Norfolk
Printed in Great Britain for Hodder & Stoughton Educational, a division of Hodder Headline Plc, 338 Euston Road, London NW1 3BH by JW Arrowsmith, Bristol.

Contents

Acknowledgements

Ian Swift would like to thank Dawn, Gary and Peter. Thanks also to all the students he has had the pleasure of teaching over the years – they make the job a joy.

Simon Harrison would like to acknowledge his parents for their ongoing support and interest, his wife Liz for her good humour and tolerance, and his cat Sinbad, for walking on the computer keyboard less than usual.

Every effort has been made to trace copyright holders but this has not always been possible in all cases; any omissions brought to our attention will be corrected in future printings.

If you have any comments on this book or suggestions for future editions, the Series Editor would be pleased to hear from you on: **gillsp@hotmail.com**

General Introduction

Using this series

This series of six books is designed specifically to develop the higher levels of skill needed for exam success and, at the same time, to provide you with a critical and detailed insight into the subject as a whole. The books are written by a team of highly experienced examiners and authors to provide you with the information and approach to achieve the best results. Whereas a traditional textbook tends to provide an explanation of topics, this series concentrates on developing ideas in a more analytical manner. When considering a topic such as location, for example, the book will focus on issues such as:

- To what extent is location a strategic decision?

- How important are qualitative factors compared to quantitative ones?

- Are location decisions less important than in the past?

- To what extent does the single currency area matter in terms of location?

- To what extent do labour costs matter?

The whole approach of the series is intended to develop a questioning and evaluative understanding of business issues. The emphasis is on why certain factors are important, rather than merely describing what they are. Reading these books will provide you with new insights into topics and help you to develop a critical view of the issues involved in the different areas of the subject.

Using this book

This particular book critically examines the management of business activity. It includes the following areas:

- location decisions

- scale of production and productivity

- stock control and just in time production

- quality

- lean production.

Throughout the text we provide up-to-date examples of business behaviour in the form of **factfiles** and **numerical investigations**. There are also numerous **progress checks** in each chapter to help you to review your understanding of the topics you have covered so far. Each chapter includes sample exam questions, students' answers (including marks awarded and marker's comments) and advice on how to answer specific types of question in the exam. Answers to the end of section questions can be found in the *Teacher's Handbook* which accompanies the series. Chapter 9 is designed to help you interpret and analyse numerical data from this syllabus area. Chapter 10 provides information on how the business concepts covered in the book are usually assessed in examinations and focuses on the key underlying issues in each topic; this will be invaluable when it comes to preparing for your exams.

Chapter 8 focuses on the most recent issues in this area of the syllabus to make sure you are completely up to date in your understanding and to provide you with the latest ideas to include in your answers.

Not only will this book provide you with a thorough understanding of the significance of the competitive and external environment of firms, it will also help you develop the approach you need to achieve top grades. It is an invaluable resource for students who want to achieve exam success.

The 'levels of response' approach to marking

In AS and A Level Business Studies candidates are assessed by their ability to demonstrate certain key skills. A student's final grade will depend on the extent to which he or she has shown the ability to analyse points, structure ideas and come to a reasoned conclusion. An A grade candidate is someone who demonstrates these skills consistently, whereas a C grade candidate shows them intermittently. To do well at A Level, students not only have to know the issues involved in each topic area, they also have to be able to develop their ideas. It is very important, therefore, that candidates provide some depth to their answers, rather than leaving many ideas undeveloped. In most cases students do better by analysing a few key points in their answers, rather than by listing many different ideas. Unfortunately, many students find it difficult to expand on their initial points; although they often demonstrate a good knowledge of the issues involved, they do not necessarily find it easy to explore these ideas further. The aim of this series of books is specifically to help you develop your ideas in more depth, which will enable you to do better in the exam.

The basic approach to assessment at AS and A Level is the same for all the examination boards and is known as 'levels of response' marking. In its simplest form this means that the mark you get depends on the skill you have demonstrated. The higher the skill shown in your answer the higher your final mark.

There are four main levels of skill assessed at A level. These are:

■ synthesis and evaluation   (the highest level skill)

■ analysis

■ explanation and application

■ identification.   (the lowest level)

As you can see the 'identification' of relevant factors is the lowest level skill. This means that listing ideas will not in itself achieve a high grade. What is important is that you explain or apply these points (i.e. show what they mean), analyse them (i.e. show why they are significant) and evaluate them (i.e. weigh up their relative importance).

In a typical question worth 9 marks, the mark scheme may look something like this:

- candidate *evaluates* relevant factors   9–7 marks
- candidate *analyses* relevant factors   6–5 marks
- candidate *explains* or applies relevant factors   4–3 marks
- candidate *identifies* relevant factors   2–1 marks

As you can see, a candidate who simply identifies factors can only achieve a maximum score of 2 out of 9. Regardless of how many different points he or she makes, if all the student has done is to list ideas they cannot get more than 2 marks in total. To move up the levels and gain more marks candidates need to demonstrate the higher level skills. Unfortunately, most textbooks spend so much time explaining ideas that they cannot do much to help develop the ability to analyse and evaluate. This series focuses throughout on these higher level skills to help you move up the levels of response in the exam and maximise your grade.

Imagine you were faced with a question which asked you to 'Discuss the factors which might determine the location of a firm'. A good answer would identify a few relevant factors, explain what is meant by them, develop their impact and then discuss their importance. For example:

'The location of an organisation may be determined by a combination of cost and demand factors. For example, a firm may need to be near its market to generate high levels of demand. This is especially true for the service sector, such as retailing: customers may be willing to travel out of their way for some goods, but in most cases a good location can have a significant impact on sales. Being close to the market may be less important in manufacturing (although distribution costs need to be considered); a firm may produce in the UK but sell worldwide.

Costs also matter because they can determine whether a location is feasible or not. Costs include the price of buying or renting land, average wages in the region and the costs of other inputs, such as energy. If a business is particularly labour intensive, for example, it may be attracted by the low wages of many developing nations. At the same time, the availability of the right skills is important – if the labour force does not have the skills, it may prove advisable to locate elsewhere.

Any location decision is likely to be based on a combination of factors (qualitative as well as quantitative) although the relative importance of each factor will vary from firm to firm. In the case of coal mining, for example, the location of the business depends primarily on the location of the actual resource; in the case of certain types of manufacturing, the labour costs may be important. In the case of scientific research, the availability of various facilities and skilled personnel may be the overriding factor.'

This a strong answer which takes a couple of points, develops them in some depth and provides some form of conclusion. For comparison, consider the following answer.

'Location depends on labour costs, availability of employees, demand, personal factors and the availability of raw materials and components.' This answer has many ideas but all of them are left undeveloped and so it is a much weaker answer.

More recent mark schemes adopt a slightly different approach in which content, application, analysis and evaluation are each given a mark, as in the example below.

CONTENT (MAX. 8 MARKS)	APPLICATION (MAX. 8 MARKS)	ANALYSIS (MAX. 8 MARKS)	EVALUATION (MAX. 16 MARKS)
8–5 marks (three or more relevant factors identified)	8–6 marks (full explanation of factors)	8–6 marks (full analysis using theory appropriately and accurately)	16–11 marks (mature judgement shown in arguments and conclusions)
4–3 marks (two relevant factors identified)	5–3 marks (some explanation of two or more factors)	5–3 marks (analysis with some use of relevant theory)	10–5 marks (judgement shown in arguments and/or conclusions)
2–1 marks (one relevant factor identified)	2–1 marks (some explanation of one factor)	2–1 marks (limited analysis of question)	4–1 marks (some judgement shown in text or conclusions)
0 marks (no knowledge shown)	0 marks (no application or explanation)	0 marks (no analysis present)	0 marks (no judgement shown)

Table 1.1 Example mark scheme

As you can see in this case (which is the mark scheme for an essay) you can gain up to 8 marks for content, 8 marks for application, 8 for analysis and 16 for evaluation. Within each category the levels approach is used so that strong evaluation can be awarded up to 16 marks, whereas more limited evaluation may only get 2 or 3 marks. The basic principles of this scheme are similar to the original levels of response model; certainly the message to candidates is clear: the higher marks require analysis and evaluation; the best marks require good analysis and evaluation! A content laden answer would only get a maximum of 8 marks.

The key to success in examinations is to consistently demonstrate the ability to analyse and evaluate – this involves exploring a few of the points you have made. All of the books in this series take an approach which should develop your critical ability and make it easier for you to discuss your ideas in more depth.

The higher level skills

What is analysis?

To analyse a point you need to show why it *matters*. Why is it relevant to the question? Why is it important? Having made a point and explained what it actually means, you need to discuss its significance either by examining what caused it or by exploring its effect on the business. This is illustrated here.

Question: *Analyse the factors which might determine how many stocks a firm holds.*

Answer: The level of stocks a firm holds may depend on the opportunity cost *(point made).* . . . This is because money invested in stocks represents funds which are tied up and could be used for something else. The firm should consider what has been sacrificed by the decision to hold stocks *(explanation).* . . . If, for example, the interest rate is high, the opportunity cost is high; the money invested in stocks could be earning a relatively high return elsewhere. The managers may try to reduce their stock levels in this situation. However, the firm will also consider the danger of running out of stocks – this could lead to a halt in production or in a failure to meet demand, which could affect customer goodwill *(analysis).*

The answer above provides a logical chain of thought: the level of stocks depends on the opportunity cost; the higher the opportunity cost the less likely the firm is to hold stocks, although demand must also be considered. Now consider a second example.

Question: *Analyse the factors which might determine whether a firm decides to expand its production.*

Answer: The decision to expand production will depend on the level of demand and the costs involved *(point made).* . . . If there is demand and the firm believes that the extra revenue will exceed any extra costs, it will be worthwhile expanding to increase profit . . . *(explanation).* Whether expanding is actually worthwhile will depend on whether the firm has to lower the price to sell more, how much more it has to spend on promotion and distribution, and whether it can benefit from economies of scale. If economies of scale exist, the cost per unit will fall as more units are produced which can increase the profit margin and make it worthwhile expanding. If, however, there are diseconomies in communication, co-ordination and control, expansion may not be worthwhile. *(analysis).*

Again the thought process is logical: the decision to expand will depend on revenue and costs; this will depend on factors such as what has to happen to the price and whether economies and diseconomies of scale exist.

What is synthesis?

Synthesis occurs when an answer is *structured effectively*. Essentially, it involves writing well organised answers rather than leaving it up to the reader to make sense of the argument. In a 'discussion' question this means putting an argument for a case, an argument against and then a conclusion.

Synthesis tends to come from planning your answer, rather than starting writing immediately. Whenever you face a question, try to sort out what you want each paragraph to say before you begin to write the answer out in full. This should lead to a better organised response. A final paragraph to bring together the arguments is also recommended.

What is evaluation?

Evaluation is the highest skill and involves demonstrating some form of *judgement*. Once you have developed various points you have to show which one or ones are most important or under what circumstances these issues are most likely to be significant. Evaluation involves some reflection on the arguments for and against and some thought about which aspects are most important. This often involves standing back from your argument to decide what would make your ideas more or less relevant. Ask yourself under what circumstances would one course of action be chosen rather than another? This process is illustrated below.

Question: *Discuss the possible gains to a firm from adopting lean production techniques.*

Answer: Lean production can improve the firm's profits *(point made)*. This is because it reduces waste, which reduces costs *(explanation)*. ... Assuming revenue does not fall, this means that profits increase. Costs fall because the firm reduces waste in terms of time taken to complete a task and the materials used up. By producing items more quickly with less inputs (but still maintaining the same standard of quality) the firm becomes more efficient and can generate higher rates of return *(analysis)*. However, lean production cannot be introduced overnight – it takes time to introduce flexible equipment and to train staff. In the short run, profits may actually fall because of the initial expense and because the cost-saving results may take time to show through. Also, lean production requires an ongoing commitment from everyone within the firm; everyone must be seeking to improve performance on an ongoing basis. It is easy for people to be very committed to begin with, but to lose interest or to identify other areas of the business which they decide are more important. If this happens, the waste can increase again. Also, employees may view requests for a greater contribution and self-checking as extra burdens; they may resist the management's attempts to introduce lean production and, so, it may not work. The success of lean production in terms of profits, therefore, depends on how it is introduced – are the benefits explained to employees and are the reward systems adjusted to encourage them to change? Over what time period is the success of these techniques being measured? It may take several years for the cost savings to occur *(evaluation of points)*.

To evaluate your arguments you need to think carefully about whether the points you have made earlier in your answer are *always* true. What makes them more or less true? What makes the impact more or less severe? To what extent can the firm avoid or exploit the situation you have described? To evaluate effectively you have to imagine different organisations and think about what factors would influence them to act in one way or another. What would make the impact of change greater or smaller? Evaluation, therefore, requires a broad appreciation of the factors which influence a firm's decisions and an awareness of the variety of organisations present in the business world.

We hope you find these books useful. They are designed to be very different from typical textbooks in that they will help you use ideas and think about their importance. At the same time, these books will provide you with new ideas about topics and, we hope, convey some of the passion and enthusiasm we have for such a fascinating subject.

CHAPTER 1

Location decisions

Does location matter?

Adecision about location may be one of the first decisions that a new business has to take, often when the manager is still inexperienced – but it may be the most important decision that is taken during a firm's lifetime. A survey by the Cranfield School of Management in 1997 found that the fastest growing small firms (in terms of revenue and profits) were also the most likely to be satisfied with their location choice.

From this, it is clear that a firm's location decision can have a major impact on its chance of success. This is because the choice of location is likely to affect both the firm's costs and its revenue.

Costs include the cost of land and labour in an area, together with transportation costs. To this extent, location has an impact on the price a firm can charge for its product. Therefore location also affects competitiveness in the marketplace. Traditional location theory looks at the combination of different costs to find the cost-minimising location.

However, costs are only one element in the location decision – the Southeast of England is the most popular business location in the UK, in spite of the fact that land prices and salaries are much higher than elsewhere in the UK. A favourable location can be an important factor in determining the level of service that can be provided to customers, therefore affecting revenue. When considering location, Jeff Bezos (founder of the Internet bookseller Amazon.com) was more concerned about the company's speed of response and access to specialist computer advice than cost – his location in Seattle combined the advantages of being an important centre for book distribution, with the widespread availability of specialist computer skills. This allowed him to offer rapid response to customer orders and to access the know-how to stay on the cutting edge of Internet technology. This has been an important part of Amazon.com's rapid growth.

KEY TERM

Shopping good
a product that consumers analyse in terms of price and quality comparison before purchase, e.g. video recorders.

The extent to which location matters also depends very much on the *type* of firm that is being considered. A good location is of vital importance for **shopping goods** retailers – the big consumer goods retailers are strongly affected by location – if customers can't see what they want, they will go elsewhere.

In the case of a **speciality good**, location is less important, because customers will be prepared to make more effort to find the particular item they want. Top-of-the-range music hardware retailers such as Bang and Olufsen, for example, do not need to locate on the high street, because they can rely on their customers to find them wherever they are.

For a firm in an industrial market, location may also be less important – much of the firm's business will be won through visits by the firm's own sales representatives to customers, rather than the other way round. Nevertheless, the further the firm's manufacturing base is from the customer, the greater the cost of transport is likely to be, possibly putting the firm at a cost disadvantage compared with other players in the market. Having said this, there is a danger of focusing overly on cost-minimisation – cutting costs in the short term by picking a very cheap location may be a serious constraint for the business in the longer term.

What makes the 'best' location?

For a profit-driven firm, the best location is one that maximises the firm's long-term income or profit stream. This tends to result from a trade-off between marketplace accessibility and cost. The nature of this trade-off depends on the sector in which the firm operates, and the nature of the business. A high street fashion chain is likely to have very different locational requirements compared to a pharmaceutical company.

A scientific approach to location choice

For many years, selecting the optimal location has been seen as a scientific decision. In principle, firms should take into account factors such as:

- the cost of land
- the resources available in an area, such as labour – average weekly earnings in the UK in 1998 ranged from £290 in Conwy (Wales) to over £500 in London
- the transport infrastructure
- access to the market
- government assistance – discretionary grants are available for firms setting up in areas of higher unemployment

These factors can be quantified using financial analysis tools and allowing the firm to make a scientific decision on the 'best' location. For example, **investment appraisal techniques** should enable the firm to work out the location with the highest rate of return, shortest payback or most favourable net present value. **Breakeven analysis** can also be applied to each site to assess its potential. As a result of all these analyses, a firm would be able to locate to an optimal site.

This scientific approach can be extended even to the not-for-profit sector, even though these organisations may have very different objectives in their location decisions than the profit-driven organisations examined above. Emergency services, for example, use 'coverage' models, so that all target areas receive attention within a given time. So, although the decision is still a scientific one, very different factors are taken into account – traffic flow and accident patterns are more relevant than labour costs and Government business grants.

Problems with the scientific approach

There are problems with this scientific approach to finding the 'best' location. Scientific analysis often plays down chance or qualitative factors. Oxfam, for instance, located in Oxford simply because that is where its founder members lived – a chance occurrence. Similarly, a low-cost location may not be optimal – firms increasingly need access to highly skilled workers, and this may well mean selecting a high-cost location. Many firms are consciously increasing their location costs by locating to business parks within easy commuting distance of major conurbations to attract top class employees.

Some location decisions are strongly influenced by the preferences of the entrepreneur – the majority of small businesses are set up near to where the entrepreneur lives, either for personal reasons (friends and family are nearby) or because of lack of access to information about other locations (**constrained optimality**). The scientific model is not able to take personal preferences into account.

The final problem with scientific location decisions is that they tend to be focused on a particular point in time – they minimise the cost using current values for wage rates, materials costs and so on. However, a location decision has an impact on the firm's success over a substantial period. If the location does not have room for expansion, or does not take account of future costs and benefits, a firm may find that a seemingly optimal location becomes rapidly suboptimal in the face of changing market conditions. The problem is that future costs and benefits are notoriously difficult to quantify. Potential changes in the marketplace are even more difficult to predict.

The larger the firm, and the longer it has been in existence, the more likely a location decision is to be scientific in nature. This is because a larger firm is likely to have more access to information about costs; it may also have experience of previous location decisions. In addition, the decision is more likely to be taken by a committee, reducing the role of individual idiosyncrasies.

The impact of technology on location

Improvements in technology have made firms in many sectors more **footloose** than they used to be. It has become easier for firms to deal with customers at a distance, thanks to the Internet and call centres. In addition, some employees are finding it less necessary to go into work every day, due to technology and the changing nature of their jobs. Consequently, a large number of firms are being forced to rethink their location strategy.

Technology in banking and insurance

From the customer's perspective, one area in which technology has had a radical impact has been in the banking and insurance market. Since First Direct and Direct Line became the early market leaders in their respective sectors, the whole nature of the way in which business is done has changed. In the 1990s Midland Bank (now HSBC) realised that the traditional branch network, opening from 9.30 am to

FACT FILE

Body Shop has made a policy of locating factories in deprived areas, rather than in the lowest-cost location. In 1988 they opened a soap factory in Easterhouse, Glasgow.

FACT FILE

Many UK call centres are located in the North of England, Scotland or Northern Ireland because the local accents are so well liked by customers.

FACT FILE

A survey by Bradford and Bingley's relocation agency ranked Aberdeen as the worst place in the UK to move a business to. West, North and East London were ranked 1, 2 and 3 – they came out top because of the size of the workforce and closeness to customers, in spite of a poor record on transport, operating costs and the low availability of premises. Source: adapted from the *Guardian* 19 September 1999

FACT FILE

In the UK, Stoke is associated traditionally with the pottery industry; Sheffield with steel; Scotland with whisky.

3.30 pm, was becoming less and less appropriate to the needs of many of its customers. The growth of families in which both partners were working meant that many people were finding it impossible to carry out their day-to-day banking business. With the improvements in 'phone and computer technology Midland Bank was able to set up First Direct. Instead of needing hundreds of expensive bank branches and local staff, First Direct operates from a call centre in Leeds. Its overheads are much lower than for traditional banks, allowing it to compete on price in the market. A similar story applies to Direct Line. Between these two companies, they have revolutionised the approach to location in their markets. Most of their competitors have been forced to follow suit, with a significant decline in the number of branch networks and a surge in the growth of telephone, and more recently Internet, banking and insurance services.

Obviously some firms are able to take fuller advantages of these technological developments than others – businesses needing physical contact with customers, or requiring a supply of raw materials will be much more restricted in their choice of location. In general, the less tangible a firm's product, the more likely it is to be able to take advantage of distance selling and service, although the growth of the Internet is making the distance selling of even quite complex tangible products – always assumed to need direct customer contact – a more and more viable operation, therefore freeing such firms from the expense of a high street location.

Teleworking

Another area in which technology has changed the parameters of location decisions is the growth of **teleworking**. Recent advances in computer technology, such as the fall in cost of **ISDN lines** and the creation of faster modems, have been matched by an increase in the numbers of people working from home. Between 1997 and 1999, the number of official teleworkers in the UK (those people working from home using a computer and telecommunications link for at least one day a week) has risen from 987,000 to 1,325,000 – an increase of over a third. Most commentators expect this trend to continue throughout the early part of the twenty-first century, some seeing it as part of a larger picture in which work is already carried out from the car and the hotel room.

The advantages of teleworking to a business are clear – with more workers out of the building, a firm can get by with a smaller office, thus freeing up valuable capital previously tied up in buildings. This can then be reinvested in the further growth of the organisation. In addition, a well developed teleworking program gives a firm access to a much wider pool of job candidates, such as people with physically disabilities or those with caring responsibilities, who might have difficulties with an office-based, 9-to-5 job.

Even the costs involved in the changeover to teleworking, such as ensuring the compatibility of home technology with that at the workplace, increased risk assessments, the provision of suitable equipment and changes to expense accounts, do not seem to be proving a significant deterrent in many sectors.

As a consequence technological developments, firms in the knowledge sector no longer need such good access to transport infrastructure. In the past, it was essential for such firms to be located in areas giving access to a pool of highly skilled technology workers – traditionally the Southeast. Increasingly however, technology workers are keen to escape the grind of office life, with a growing number moving house to areas such as Scotland and teleworking from there. The advantages to the employee are clear – less stress from a daily commute and effectively shorter working hours. If this trend continues, firms may need to reassess their location priorities – they may find that they can operate with much smaller premises and in a lower cost location.

Country	% of workforce
Finland	16.8
Sweden	15.2
Netherlands	14.5
Denmark	10.5
UK	7.6
Germany	6.0
Ireland	4.4
Italy	3.6
France	2.9
Spain	2.8

Source: ECATT survey (funded by the European Commission, DG XIII), 1999, quoted in *People Management* 25 November 1999

Table 1.1 Teleworkers in the EU (1999)

The logical extension of the teleworking trend is for businesses to have no location at all! Networks of knowledge workers, such as accountants and IT professionals are beginning to build up around the country. These networked workers have a central co-ordinator. Firms wanting a particular service 'phone the co-ordinator who gets in touch with the nearest available contractor – such networks are able to offer highly competitive rates because of their virtually non-existent overheads. In some ways this is simply an extension of the ideas behind First Direct and Direct Line – why have a location at all if it isn't necessary?

In conclusion, technology seems likely to have an impact on the location decisions of the future – teleworking seems set to grow, and increasing numbers of firms are marketing their services over the Internet and the 'phone, altering the nature of location decisions.

Problems with teleworking

There may be hidden costs involved in the change to teleworking that may only become apparent over the years. Some homeworkers, although eliminating one type of stress, are becoming stressed by the constant need to self-motivate and to separate home from work. Managers will have to develop new skills in order to communicate and deal effectively with subordinates they rarely meet face-to-face.

Overall, the rapid change in the technological environment is having a major impact on the location and strategic decisions of a large number of firms. It has been estimated that by 2010 50% of the working population will be doing at least

some of their work from home. Coupled with the extraordinary growth of Internet selling, it is clear that many firms will have to review their need to be close to either the market or to their core employees, adding a whole new dimension to the location decision.

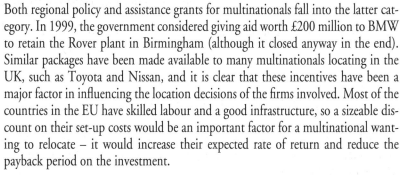

PROGRESS CHECK

Discuss the ways in which the growth of teleworking might affect a firm's location decision.

Government influence on location decisions

Over the years, different Governments have made many attempts to influence the location of businesses, partly because of differential employment patterns across the UK and partly for environmental reasons. The government of the day can influence firms in two basic ways – either by preventing location in certain areas, or by making other areas more attractive.

Do government grants attract businesses?

Both regional policy and assistance grants for multinationals fall into the latter category. In 1999, the government considered giving aid worth £200 million to BMW to retain the Rover plant in Birmingham (although it closed anyway in the end). Similar packages have been made available to many multinationals locating in the UK, such as Toyota and Nissan, and it is clear that these incentives have been a major factor in influencing the location decisions of the firms involved. Most of the countries in the EU have skilled labour and a good infrastructure, so a sizeable discount on their set-up costs would be an important factor for a multinational wanting to relocate – it would increase their expected rate of return and reduce the payback period on the investment.

This type of government assistance is generally made as a one-off payment; it helps to offset the initial set-up costs, but given that a location decision will have an impact on a firm's profits over many years, the assistance may be less important than it might appear at first.

Some commentators have suggested that multinationals are simply playing regions and countries off against one another – that having decided on their preferred location, they try to extract as much aid as possible.

Assistance is also available for smaller firms. Regional aid packages in the form of Regional Selective Assistance provide £100 to 140 million a year in total for small scale projects.

It can be argued that packages of this nature have a major impact on location decisions by cutting a businesses initial set-up costs as they do. However, in the case of multinationals, it is difficult to know whether the location decision would have been without the assistance. Rather than influencing a location decision, perhaps the government is simply boosting the profitability of these firms.

Planning regulations can prevent location in certain areas

The second way in which the government can influence firms' location decisions is by preventing location in certain areas. Since the 1997 General Election the government has moved against out-of-town shopping developments, arguing that they increase car usage and that they damage small businesses in and around town centres leading to a reduction in choice for those without cars.

Since it is not possible to build these new shopping developments without planning permission, the government has been able to dramatically alter the location decisions of the leading supermarket chains, forcing them to rethink their entire expansion strategy.

Therefore, the government wields both a carrot and stick when it comes to location decisions. Whilst the effectiveness of the stick is fairly clear – outright planning prevention is just that. As we have seen, the impact of the carrot is less clear because it is so difficult to know what proportion of businesses are affected by the offer of government assistance.

PROGRESS CHECK

To what extent can the government influence a firm's location decision?

Is relocation a good option?

KEY TERM

A greenfield site is one which was previously undeveloped.

In the late 1980s and early 1990s, a common driving force behind relocation was an attempt to cut costs by moving out of expensive city centre offices to low-cost, often government-subsidised, greenfield sites.

These decisions have backfired on a number of companies due to unforeseen factors. Donald Andrews, head of Corporate Real Estate at Laporte welcomed the organisation's decision to move back to London, from a low-cost facility in Luton. His view is that:

> 'The company needed to be seen as a go-getter and culturally agile. Luton was an entirely inappropriate location; the only time there was any social interaction was when someone was leaving ... we know a lot more about each other now.'

Problems have also been encountered by companies with a large number of international clients – 'low-cost' locations such as Milton Keynes and South Wales may have hidden costs in terms of transport and lost contracts, as they are some distance from Gatwick and Heathrow.

FACT FILE

The relocation of GCHQ (the security services listening headquarters) from one side of Cheltenham to another cost over £300 m; the devices which listen in to communications all over the world could not be turned off at any time during the move.

KEY TERM

Industrial or locational inertia

a situation in which a firm is located in an area but the original reasons for the location are no longer relevant. The firm remains because of the expense and difficulty of relocation or the build up of intangible (non-quantifiable) benefits which may outweigh the tangible costs of poor location.

KEY POINTS

Relocation is more likely to be successful if:

- staff are footloose
- it is not seen simply as a cost-cutting exercise
- the firm is not dependent on the 'buzz', contacts or image of a big city
- it is used as one part of a change program.

As a consequence, a number of organisations are moving back to major city centres, often citing a lack of 'buzz' in their previous location as the reason – 'buzz' is an intangible factor that is difficult to incorporate into location versus cost decisions.

The receipe for success?

Firms that have made a success of relocation seem to be those that have used the move as an opportunity to generate cultural change. The Defence Procurement Executive, for example, used its move to Bristol as a chance to change the entire culture of the organisation. The agency moved to purpose-built, open-plan offices which won awards for design communications, décor and energy use. What made the relocation a success though, was the extensive staff consultation process, and the desire to change the culture of the organisation from one in which 14 different sites competed, to an informal and open culture of co-operation.

The message seems to be that relocation is more likely to be a success if staff can see it as more than just a cost-cutting exercise – not surprising given implications for staff faced with personal relocation or redundancy. In addition, many organisations have used relocation as an opportunity to update their IT facilities, negotiate with unions, or change working conditions; all factors that affect staff but that are difficult to quantify.

Reasons for not relocating

It is the associated costs of relocation that cause many firms to stay put, even when the original reasons for a particular location are long gone. One of the best known examples of this **industrial inertia** is the steel industry in Sheffield. The industry located there in the nineteenth century because of the abundance of limestone, coal and iron ore. Many of these raw materials are now shipped in from as far away as Australia, which would make a port a more logical location. However, the costs of relocating would be enormous, easily offsetting the benefit of lower transportation costs. In addition, the area has a reputation for quality steel production, which provides an incentive to stay in a high-cost location.

Another important factor might be the ethics of a relocation decision. In certain areas a local community may become dependent on a firm for employment. If the firm were to relocate, the decision could have a devastating impact on one of the firm's major stakeholder groups – the employees, who might be unable or unwilling to relocate with the firm.

The key problem making relocation decisions is assessing the non-quantifiable elements. It is relatively easy to see in quantifiable terms which location will be best in terms of minimising transport costs, and so on. It is harder to judge the message that the firm will send out to employees, customers and other stakeholders by relocating. This is why location and relocation decisions are so fraught with difficulties.

PROGRESS CHECK

Discuss the possible reasons why a firm might decide to relocate.

Globalisation and location

The international location decisions of multinational companies are becoming increasingly important. The world's 1000 largest companies account for 80% of the world's industrial output, and their decisions to locate in a particular country or region can have a major impact on the economy of that area. In 1998–1999, for example, foreign direct investment into the UK created 44,413 jobs and safeguarded (through the purchase of failing domestic firms) a further 74,430.

This trend towards globalisation means that both developed and developing countries have an increasing number of foreign-owned companies locating within their borders. There are several reasons for this:

- Producing and selling within one market reduces the impact of exchange rate movements – companies such as Sony have balanced their location and production decisions so that their exports and imports are roughly equivalent.

- Multinationals seek to avoid the protectionist policies of the major trading blocs, such as the EU, by locating within them. It was the very restrictive quotas imposed by the EU that caused the first wave of Japanese car manufacturers to locate in the UK in the 1970s and 1980s. Even following the recent round of trade negotiations in Uruguay which were aimed at reducing protectionism, many barriers to trade still exist.

- Many multinationals have sought to gain competitive advantage through reduced production costs, by locating in developing countries, where wage rates are much lower than in the developed world. Nevertheless, although wages are lower, some firms, especially technology firms, have found that quality can be a problem.

- Multinationals are attracted by substantial government grants – up to a third of the set-up costs in the UK can be met by a combination of EU and UK grants, giving a substantial boost to the profitability of an investment.

Cultural differences

Multinationals often face problems associated with language and culture differences between countries, especially if different countries are producing different parts of the same product. The new Eurofighter jet, for example, will be built in Germany, Spain, Italy and Warton, near Preston in Lancashire. Of the main components, one wing will be Spanish, the other will be Italian, the cockpit will be British and the fuselage German. A key problem according to Wolfram Nitsch, the Human Resources Director of Eurofighter, is that the official language is English, requiring all participants to be fluent.

> 'The southern Europeans feel disadvantaged,' according to Nitsch. 'The Spanish especially will not admit that they haven't understood something – they simply agree. And you have to be sensitive to varying language skills.'

Language problems are not the only difficulties faced by Eurofighter though; the decision-making process of each country's managers is also different. Whereas the

FACT FILE

Since 1991 Kent has been part of the Euroregion, a formal alliance with Brussels, Flanders, Wallonia and Nord-Pas de Calais. The regions promote one another's tourist attractions, organise school exchanges, and are planning to market themselves as a single business location to Asian investors.
Source: *Financial Times* 15 December 1999

Southern Europeans tend to need consensus and social contact to build up trust before decisions are made, the Germans and British are more empowered to take immediate decisions. As a result, the decision-taking process can be quite slow, creating frustrations. In spite of this, the project is generally regarded as a success, partly due to the internal awareness of exactly the problems mentioned. Without such awareness, it is likely that serious problems could arise.

Despite the potential problems, the trend towards globalisation is likely to continue, and that growth will not just be in manufacturing – direct foreign investment into the UK in the non-manufacturing sector (especially financial services and telecommunications) rose by 141% between 1994 and 1998. So, for most large firms, location seems to have become an international rather than a national issue.

PROGRESS CHECK

Discuss the possible reasons why the UK has attracted so much foreign investment in recent years.

The impact of the euro on location decisions

Does non-membership matter?

An important issue is how much influence the UK's decision on entry into the European single currency will have on international location decisions. This is particularly relevant because in 2000 the UK was the number one choice for direct foreign investment in the EU.

COUNTRY	%
UK	23.0
France	14.6
Belgium/Luxembourg	12.0
Germany	11.5
Netherlands	10.7

Table 1.2 Direct Foreign Investment in the EU, by % of total stock

FACT FILE

In November 1998, Toyota announced a £350 million investment in Valenciennes in France, rather than investing further in its plant in Derby, in spite of a plea from the British government to reconsider. Its aim was to be at the heart of the euro area.

During the last few months of 1999, several leading car manufacturers went on record as saying they would have to reconsider their investments if the UK was not to join the single currency in the next 2 to 3 years. On 17 January 2000, Syoichiro Toyoda, Honorary Chairman of Toyota, threatened to pull out of the UK if the government did not set an early timetable for joining. At this point, Toyota had already invested £1.5 billion in the UK. His threat followed similar warnings from Fiat, Ford and BMW.

The basic question facing these firms is whether the UK's non-membership of the euro imposes significant enough costs to outweigh the advantages of locating in the UK. The obvious costs of remaining outside the euro area are the costs of currency conversion, together with the risk of adverse exchange rate movements.

For firms selling mostly in mainland Europe, these costs could be eliminated simply by producing there. Vauxhall has estimated that non-membership of the euro is costing it £10 million a year, and in 2000 most UK exporters were being hit by the strength of the pound. These problems would not exist if the UK were to enter the single currency.

The central issue is whether the costs of non-membership are significant enough to deter location in the UK. Some commentators have pointed out that it is mainly car manufacturers who have done most of the complaining, and their industry is notoriously competitive, making the costs of non-membership more significant to them.

Ford UK, for example, made profits of just $28 million (£17 million) in 1999, a profit margin of 0.09% – clearly currency conversion costs are more worrying to a firm in this situation than to one with a healthier profit margin.

FACT FILE

Over a fifth of investment into the EU flows into the UK.

Do the advantages outweigh the disadvantages?

The reasons that the UK has been such a popular investment area seem to be more to do with language, culture, availability of skills (especially in computer software and telecommunications), and relatively low labour costs compared with France and Germany.

These advantages are clearly quite significant – a low-cost, skilled workforce speaking the international language of business – and some commentators think they easily outweigh the disadvantages of currency conversion, which is not a new cost. There is some support for this view, in that inward investment into the UK reached record levels in 1998, when the pound was already strong, suggesting that currency fluctuations are not a key factor in international location decisions, and that membership of the single currency may not be a very significant factor influencing location decisions.

The ethics of international location

Exploitation of developing nations or wealth creation?

Much of the debate over multinationals' business strategies has focused on their movement into developing economies; at the end of the twentieth century there were major investments into both Eastern Europe and the Pacific rim. On the one hand these companies seem to be generating wealth and foreign currency earnings for the countries in which they locate; on the other they are accused of exploitation.

In January 1997, for example, an internal report prepared by Ernst and Young for Nike on the firm's factories in Vietnam was leaked to Dara O'Rourke, an environmental consultant for the UN Industrial Development Organisation. This report found that employees were working 65 hour weeks for $10 and also detailed poor working conditions, with some factories containing carcinogens that exceeded local permitted levels by up to 177 times.

Before his execution in 1995, the author Ken Saro-Wiwa campaigned vigorously against what he claimed were the irresponsible actions of Shell against Ogoni tribespeople in Nigeria.

In 1999, the *Independent* newspaper began a campaign against sweatshops, running stories about low wages and poor conditions in factories operated by firms such as The Gap in the Pacific rim.

Multinationals such as Shell and Nike dispute these claims, arguing that they are wealth creators – without their presence, there would be lower employment, and the countries would be unable to make use of resources such as oil reserves, because they would lack the technology and expertise to exploit them.

Most multinationals also argue that they stick to local agreements on minimum wages and conditions, even if these are very different from what might be expected in the developed world. There is also evidence that multinationals are not necessarily poor payers – a recent OECD survey suggests that in Turkey wages paid by foreign firms are 124% above the average.

FACT FILE

The stock of foreign-owned assets in the UK was $270 billion by 1998.

Tax issues

A different argument centres around tax evasion. Some firms are using the opportunity to be internationally footloose to move their corporate headquarters to places such as Bermuda and the Cayman Islands where tax levels are much lower than in the major industrial nations. This pressure, it is argued, has kept down taxes on companies in the industrialised nations, so that in many countries, taxes on corporate income are lower than taxes on personal income.

The power of the multinational

The problem with multinationals is that they are perceived to be both very powerful and difficult to control, meaning that they can put enormous pressure even on the governments of rich, developed economies, as seen by the threats made by firms over the UK's entry into the single currency. If multinationals wield such power in the developed world, what does this mean for poorer developing countries?

The counterargument is that pressure groups and other non-government organisations (NGOs) are becoming increasingly strong and well financed, allowing them to act as a check on the actions of multinationals. In addition, the growth of the Internet is allowing information to be spread more quickly and widely than ever before, allowing consumers to make a more informed choice about products.

Certainly, in developed countries, with well-informed consumers and an independent legal system, there is probably little to fear from multinationals locating in the country. In the developing world, where these conditions may not be met, the case is less clear-cut.

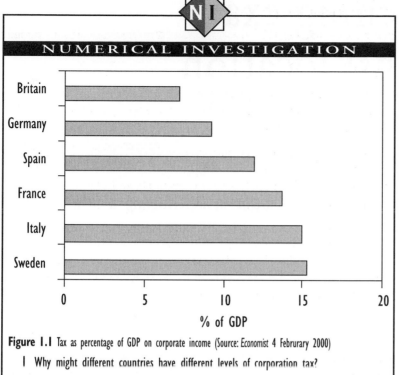

Figure 1.1 Tax as percentage of GDP on corporate income (Source: *Economist* 4 Februrary 2000)

1 Why might different countries have different levels of corporation tax?

2 Discuss how significant these figures might be for a multinational manufacturer thinking of locating in the EU.

Summary chart

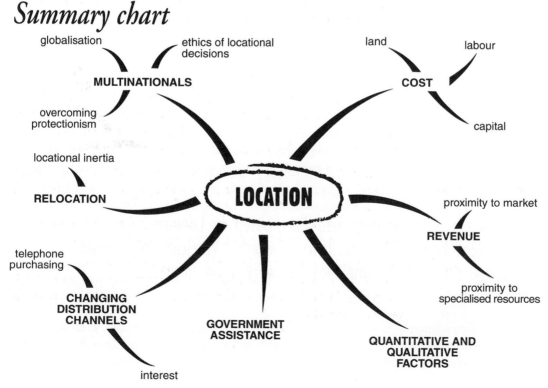

Figure 1.2 Location decisions

Approaching exam questions: location decisions

Discuss whether location is the key factor in determining a firm's success.

(11 marks)

The first thing to do when answering this question is to look for the important phrases in the question. In this case they are 'the key factor', 'success' and 'a firm'. The temptation for many candidates will be to explain generally why location is important, without evaluating the *extent* to which it matters, and whether it will be the same for all firms.

Some of the points that a strong candidate would address include:

■ Is the firm in the service sector or in manufacturing? Location will affect firms in each sector differently. The usual argument is that it will matter more for service sector firms due to the need for contact with the customer. A strong candidate would make this argument, but would look for counterexamples in, say, banking and the financial services.

■ If it is a manufacturing firm, what type? There is no such thing as a homogenous 'manufacturing' firm. Some have more need for access to technology skills than others, in which case location may become critical.

■ Is it a location-dependent firm? For some firms, location will be the key factor in determining whether they succeed. Mining firms need ore deposits, for example.

■ Is it the *key* factor? Whilst location may be more important for some firms than others, this still does not mean it is necessarily the key factor. The most important factor may be the firm's product, other firms in the industry, or a whole host of other factors in combination.

■ Will it determine the firm's success? The importance of location may depend on the definition of success. For a small firm run by an entrepreneur wanting to provide jobs for his or her home town, location may well be the key factor.

Woricker plc is a medium-sized firm, based in London, offering independent financial advice. Discuss whether Woricker plc should encourage more of its employees to work from home.

(11 marks)

There is too little information in this question to be able to come to any firm conclusions, so the best answers will use an 'it depends' approach. This will involve identifying and explaining the key factors that would make teleworking a more or less workable option for the firm. When answering in this way, however, it is vital to avoid the classic weak 'it depends' answer. This identifies a well-learned list of factors on which anything might depend, and then churns them out without any explanation or reference to the context.

The sort of factors that might be relevant here are:

- If the firm gives most of its financial advice in written form, over the 'phone or in person.
- If enough employees are likely to be interested to make the exercise worthwhile.
- If the firm has the IT facilities and support to make the project viable.
- If there are potential benefits in terms of reduced size of premises.
- If the firm is short of space in its current location.

In spite of rapid changes in technology, communications and transport infrastructure, many firms remain in the same location in which they first set up. Discuss possible reasons why this might be the case.

(11 marks)

As ever, it is important to avoid falling into the trap of talking about firms in general. It is important to remember that the vast majority of firms are, in fact, very small – they are often approximately the same size as when they started. Changes in communication, technology and infrastructure often matter less to small, service-based firms employing only a handful of employees.

The key to the answer is that firms are unlikely to relocate unless there is a pressing reason to do so, because the process is so expensive. A good answer, having dealt with the 'type of firm' issue, will move on to look at the different costs that might be incurred when relocating. These will include:

- The cost of recruiting and training new staff.
- The cost of informing customers of the move.
- The cost of buying, moving into and converting new premises.

A strong answer would deal briefly with the reasons why firms move in spite of these costs (desire for culture change, running out of space etc.), thereby turning the question neatly around on itself.

F7 is a multinational company wishing to set up a factory employing 1500 people in the UK, in exchange for a contribution to set-up costs of £500 million. Discuss the factors the government might consider when coming to a decision about this proposal.

(11 marks)

This is a fairly straightforward question, and the only problem will be for candidates who fail to look at both sides and come to a balanced conclusion. Here too there will be an element of 'it depends', because the question says nothing about the *type* of firm involved, and it will be important to make reference to the figure of £500 million.

Points in favour of making the grant should include:

- Creation of jobs, depending on the current state of the job market.

- The multiplier effect stemming from the initial job creation.

- The impact on the balance of payments (if the goods are exported).

- The introduction of new management techniques and technology (depending on the type of jobs created).

Points against might include:

- The damage to local firms competing in the same market (if there are any, and if they would be damaged).

- The reputation of the multinational as an employer (could be a point in favour in some cases).

- Whether the multinational is likely to avoid paying tax in the host country.

- What else could be done with £500 million?

- Would the company come anyway?

Finally, there is a necessity to come to a conclusion, which should summarise the circumstances under which the government should and should not get involved, with reasons.

Student answers

Analyse the circumstances under which a firm might consider introducing a teleworking programme.

(9 marks)

Student answer

Teleworking means getting some of your workers to do work from home. The advantage to the firm is that it will save space, meaning that it can move to a cheaper location. If the firm was expanding too fast, it might give them time to find a bigger factory.

The problem is that some people cannot be trusted to work from home, because you do not know what they are doing – there is nothing to make them get up on time and start work. This could reduce productivity which would increase costs and decrease profits. The firm might become bankrupt in the long run.

Also, the decision to introduce such a scheme depends on whether the firm has good computing equipment. People will need to send in work by the Internet. If the firm does not have the necessary technology it will be inefficient.

Therefore, the firm should only introduce teleworking if it has good IT.

Marker's comments

This is a moderate answer that fails to answer the question directly. The first paragraph deals with the advantages of teleworking, which is not really what the question is asking. Nevertheless, the candidate turns it around by talking about the need for space as a likely circumstance in which the introduction of teleworking might be likely.

The second paragraph is quite weak, exposing the candidate's lack of understanding about how the business world actually works. The initial argument is very simplistic, and the part about productivity is clearly a well learned argument that scores little because there is no explanation of the chain of reasoning.

The final paragraph is relevant again, but focuses only on the simplistic computer resources issue of teleworking.

Mark: Content 2/2, Application, 1/3, Analysis 1/4. Total = 4

Discuss how significant the single currency is likely to be for location decisions in the twenty-first century

(12 marks)

Student answer

The single currency, or euro, means that those countries taking part will avoid any problems with transaction costs from converting currencies, and also there will be no risk of losing out because of currency appreciation or depreciation. This should make location in the euro area more attractive for a firm wishing to sell in other euro area countries – they will be able to sell in the same currency that they pay their costs, which also makes planning easier. An example of the impact this might have is illustrated by British firms at the moment, complaining that the strength of the pound is making them uncompetitive in world markets; if the UK was a member of the euro zone, this would not be an issue (unless we had entered at the current rate). Therefore, the single currency could have quite a big impact on location decisions.

On the other hand, it is not the only factor – the availability of skills, raw materials and so on are also very important. Especially given changes in technology, firms need to be able to get the computing skills that they need, and this is why Britain is still quite a popular location in spite of the strong pound.

Marker's comments

This answer starts off very well – a quick definition of what is meant by the euro, and then a very detailed account of its significance. The candidate also looks at the other side of the argument in the second paragraph, although this seems rather rushed, implying that too much time was spent on the first part. This means that the candidate has not had time to bring the argument to a conclusion, which will limit its evaluation mark, although the comment about the UK entry rate into the euro shows some evidence of judgement, and would be rewarded.

Mark: Content 2/2, Application & Analysis 5/6, Evaluation 1/3. Total = 8

Discuss whether a country should welcome a multinational firm wanting to set up a factory that would create 1500 jobs.

(12 marks)

Student answer

Much will depend on the type of multinational, the type of industry and the type of country.

Some multinationals can be very bad for a country, by exploiting the workforce, e.g. Guess in the US. The country should not welcome this type of firm because it would break laws and exploit the workers. But 1500 jobs are quite a lot. If the economy is really suffering, then it might be worth it, since some jobs would be better than none.

The type of industry would matter. If the country already had its own firms, then the multinational might be so big that it would wipe out the country's industry, causing job losses, maybe even more than the multinational created. Then if the multinational was to go away again, the country would have no industry at all.

Finally, developing countries have a hard choice, because often they need the jobs. But the multinational is often bigger than the country itself – e.g. 10 multinationals have sales bigger than the Australian government's tax revenue. This means that they might not obey the law, and because they are so powerful, the developing country may not be able to do too much about it. In a developed country this might not be so bad, because they could sue the multinational and stop it.

Marker's comments

This is a very difficult answer to mark. The candidate has clearly been well taught, from the 'it depends' in the first paragraph, to the clear structure of the answer, and the use of examples to sup-

port the points made. The problem is that the language used is very weak, and the points are often explained in too simple a manner, especially given the complex nature of the topic.

Evaluation is very limited, possibly some credit being awarded for the two-sided nature of the first and third paragraphs. There is analysis, but the mark suffers because of the way the points are explained – it's all too definite.

Mark: Content 2/2, Application & Analysis 3/6, Evaluation 1/3. Total = 6

Analyse the possible reasons behind the growth of out-of-town supermarkets during the 1980s.

(9 marks)

In the 1980s lots of people had more cars and the economy was doing really well. This meant that everybody wanted to buy more and better things, which meant that the supermarkets were not good enough. So more had to be built. But there was no space in the town centres and it was too expensive anyway. So they built them on the edge of town, which might have been bad, but because the economy was doing so well everybody had cars so they were able to get there. The city centre supermarkets were all shut, which was bad for people who did not have cars because they had to go to corner shops which are more expensive, and if you do not have a car, then you are poor anyway.

Overall, in conclusion the big out-of-town supermarkets were built because everybody had cars and lots of money because the economy was so good.

Marker's comments

This is the classic 'panic' answer of a candidate who is really nervous. He or she has some ideas, but completely fails to structure the answer. As a result the points tumble over one another, and are never really developed properly. With more structure, and more time spent on the main points, the answer could have been quite good.

Mark: Content 1/2, Application 1/3, Analysis 0/4. Total = 2

End of section questions

1 Analyse the possible reasons why the UK is the most popular destination for multinational location in the EU.

(9 marks)

2 To what extent is government assistance likely to influence a firm's location decisions?

(11 marks)

3 Analyse the likely impact of the growth in home Internet access on the location decisions of firms.

(9 marks)

4 Evaluate the likely costs and benefits to a firm of allowing more employees to work some of their hours from home.

(11 marks)

5 Discuss the likely benefits to a financial services firm of a move out of a city centre to a greenfield site.

(11 marks)

6 Analyse the possible reasons for London's continuing popularity as a business location.

(9 marks)

7 A company's prime raw material is available at a coastal location, however their main customer base is situated inland. What factors will be most important when determining their choice of location?

(11 marks)

8 Discuss the circumstances that might make a firm consider relocation.

(11 marks)

9 Analyse the factors that make some firms more 'footloose' than others.

(9 marks)

10 Discuss the extent to which the factors influencing the location of a new primary school might differ from those of a steel foundry.

(11 marks)

Essays

1 A rapidly expanding manufacturing company needs to find more factory space (unavailable at their current site), but the goods they are making require highly specialised skills which the firm itself has developed locally over many years. Evaluate the possible options facing the firm in its attempts to resolve this situation.

(40 marks)

2 There is no such thing as an optimal location. Discuss.

(40 marks)

3 'The availability of specialist skills is the key factor in location decisions in the twenty-first century.' To what extent do you agree with this statement?

(40 marks)

4 'A good product is far more important than a good location.' How far do you agree with this assertion?

(40 marks)

5 'Multinationals locate in developing countries to exploit the fact that there is often less regulation of the impact of their activities on the environment and the way they treat labour.' Discuss.

(40 marks)

CHAPTER 2
Productivity

Introduction

Productivity is a measure of the output produced per unit of input. Productivity is critically important to a firm since it affects the cost per unit. The higher the level of productivity the lower the cost per unit, other things being equal. To be competitive, managers seek to increase productivity.

The average level of productivity in the UK has been a serious cause of concern to successive UK governments. In most of the Budgets of the late twentieth and early twenty-first centuries, the UK government has announced policies designed to increase productivity and stimulate innovation. One possible reason for this has been the productivity gap which exists between the UK and other leading world economies. Whereas in the 1950s the UK's labour productivity was higher than France and Germany, but lower than the US, the UK now trails all three. This means that UK firms are likely to be uncompetitive relative to their international competitors.

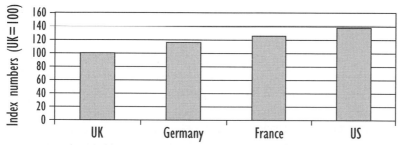

Figure 2.1 Output per worker (1998) (Source: OECD)

Production is the total amount of output. Productivity is the output per unit of input.

Measuring productivity

Productivity can be defined as the output produced per period of time divided by inputs. However, this definition simplifies what is actually a very complex problem, because outputs and inputs and the relationship between them can be difficult to measure.

KEY TERM

Productivity
$$\frac{\text{Output per period of time}}{\text{Quantity of input used}}$$

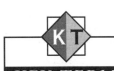

KEY TERM

Total factor productivity
measures output in relation to the total inputs.

FACT FILE

Labour productivity rose by 241% in Thailand between 1980 and 1996 compared with 30% in the UK and only 22% in the US.

KEY POINTS

Productivity is easier to measure:

- where output is easy to measure (e.g. in manufacturing rather than in services)
- the more direct the factors' contribution to output (e.g. production line workers rather than support staff)
- the fewer the changes in the quality of output over time
- the more consistent the quality of inputs across the business and industry.

At one end of the scale, the labour productivity of production line workers is fairly easy to measure – the workers have a direct impact on a measurable output. Even then though, there is a debate about whether it should be *units* of output or the *value* of output that should be measured. If the simpler units-based approach is used, there is still a problem in making inter-industry comparisons if one firm is making a higher quality product than another.

PROGRESS CHECK

Two businesses produce 1000 tyres a day. Firm A's tyres last 15,000 miles. Firm B however uses 10% more labour and materials to make tyres that last 40,000 miles. Which firm has the higher productivity?

The problems are even more difficult when trying to include or measure the productivity of support staff, who do not impact directly on output – engineers, supervisors and Human Resource managers all make significant indirect contributions to productivity, but it is difficult to measure this exactly. Similarly, the output of service sector organisations like the Benefits agency or the NHS is difficult to measure precisely – in the latter case, patients dealt with per employee could be a possible measure, but there are many different types of patient – a long-term in-patient takes far more time and attention than a once-a-month out-patient.

PROGRESS CHECK

How might a school measure its productivity?

A further problem can arise from focusing too much on one type of productivity (such as output per worker). For example, an easy way to increase labour productivity is to increase the amount of machinery available by investing in capital. Each worker will make more, but whether the firm's overall productivity rises will depend on what happened to its capital productivity as well. Labour and capital productivity are interrelated, making measurement difficult. As a result, organisations such as the International Labour Organisation now stress the importance of looking at **total factor productivity** as the key measure.

PROGRESS CHECK

How can output fall but productivity increase?

How important is productivity?

Given the emphasis that UK governments have placed on improving productivity, there is obviously an extent to which productivity is very important both for an individual firm and the economy as a whole. Even if productivity cannot be accurately measured, there are still benefits to be derived from increasing it.

One of the main reasons that productivity matters is its impact on international competitiveness. Given equivalent wage rates and quality etc., a firm that can make

20 units per hour will have lower unit costs than a firm that can only make 10 units per hour. This will give it substantial benefits in the marketplace. One obvious consequence would be that the more productive firm could undercut its rivals' prices, increasing value for money, and having a major impact on both revenue and profit in price elastic markets.

If the market is not very price sensitive, the firm may leave price unchanged and use

NUMERICAL INVESTIGATION

NUMBER OF EMPLOYEES	OUTPUT (UNITS)	LABOUR PRODUCTIVITY	WEEKLY WAGE COSTS (IF WAGE RATE = £300 PER WEEK)	LABOUR COST PER UNIT (£)
60	3000	50	1500	0.50
120	?	50	?	?
180	12000	?	?	?
240	24000	?	?	?

Table 2.1 Calculating productivity

1 Copy out the table above and calculate the missing figures.
2 Comment on the relationship between productivity and unit labour costs.

the lower costs to increase profits per unit. These profits can be reinvested into research and development, or capital equipment, which should further increase productivity and competitiveness in the long term, providing the investments are sound.

For the economy as a whole, higher productivity means that UK firms may be more competitive abroad, helping to boost exports and improve the **balance of payments**. Rising export demand may lead to an increase in the number of jobs, although rising productivity, especially labour productivity, may offset some of the employment gains (because fewer employees will be needed to make the same output).

Nevertheless, there are those who argue that productivity is only part of the answer both for firms and the economy as a whole. The productivity gains in the UK in the late 1990s and early 2000s, for example, only had a limited impact on UK firms' competitiveness because of the strength of sterling – the pound was a third higher in 2000 than it was following the UK's exit from the ERM in 1992 – productivity gains were nowhere near this much, reducing UK firms' international competitiveness.

A further point is that productivity is only one part of the cost equation – the wages paid to employees are also very important. In the UK, hourly compensation costs in 1998 averaged $16.43 compared with $18.56 in the US, $20.47 for the EU as a whole and $27.20 in Germany. Therefore, although the UK has lower labour productivity, it also has lower labour costs (partly due to the more flexible labour force in the UK, and the comparative lack of employment legislation) meaning that the cost disadvantage is dramatically reduced.

PROGRESS CHECK

Morgan Cars produces less than 15 cars a week from a substantial workforce. Analyse the possible reasons why the firm can survive despite such low productivity.

The benefits and disadvantages of high productivity depend on how it has been brought about. If it has been achieved by cutting corners on quality, or by slashing jobs and increasing pressure on the remaining workers, the gains may only be short term. In the longer term, the firm is likely to lose market share to higher quality alternatives (especially during a period of economic growth), and labour turnover is likely to rise as employees leave to look for better jobs, increasing recruitment and training costs, and ultimately damaging productivity.

Finally, the government itself has stated that productivity is only a means to an end. Gordon Brown (the Chancellor of the Exchequer) has argued that productivity by itself may encourage firms to look too much to the short term, and that long-term competitive advantage lies in knowledge and innovation, rather than simply being more productive.

Productivity can have an immediate impact on competitiveness, but in the longer term, competitiveness will come from innovation and entrepreneurship – there is little point in being productive at making things that people no longer want. In today's dynamic and fast growing sectors, the ability to adapt quickly to change may be more important than static productivity.

FACT FILE

Peter Mandelson at the CBI conference in 1998 said, 'Knowledge is the only source of competitive advantage. Brainpower is more important than brawn, intelligence more powerful than energy, creativity more critical than raw materials.'

KEY POINTS

Productivity is less important in determining competitiveness:

- the less price sensitive the market is
- the more it is prone to technological change
- the more difficult it is to measure
- the less other factors have been compromised to achieve it
- the greater the significance of other factors in determining competitiveness.

NUMERICAL INVESTIGATION

COUNTRY	INDEX OF LABOUR PRODUCTIVITY IN MANUFACTURING, 1996 (UK = 100)	INDEX OF HOURLY COMPENSATION COSTS (BASED ON US DOLLARS) FOR PRODUCTION WORKERS IN MANUFACTURING, 1996† (UK = 100)
US	171	125
France	130	147
Germany	126	214
Japan	147	148

† Gap has narrowed considerably since 1996

Table 2.2 Country index of labour productivity in manufacturing (Source: Mary O'Mahoney, NIESR 1999 and US Dept. of Labour, Bureau of Labour Statistics, January 2000)

1 Which country appears to be the most competitive in manufacturing in 1996?
2 Analyse the other factors that are likely to have an impact on international competitiveness.
3 Discuss whether the table implies that German firms will be unable to compete in world markets.

Key factors determining productivity

Assuming that we are looking at total factor productivity (i.e. ensuring that the firm makes best use of all its inputs rather than focusing on just one), there are several important influences to consider.

Quality of inputs

One of the most important factors is the quality of the inputs used. If labour is better trained and equipment is more up to date, then output per factor is likely to be higher. Investment in the training of employees can have both direct and indirect benefits – a direct benefit is that a trained worker is likely to carry out their work more efficiently, therefore getting more done. An indirect benefit may be that workers feel more valued, helping the firm to retain a well-trained workforce, and minimising the disruption caused by continually integrating new employees into the workforce. One of the problems facing UK firms in particular is that the UK workforce is less skilled on average than its continental rivals – for example 22% of UK workers have poor literacy skills, 50% more than the equivalent figure in Germany.

FACT FILE

A recent study report that 70% of employees admit to taking naps at work, and what's more it raises productivity! Some companies have introduced sleeping rooms in their offices, and have found an increase in productivity and a reduction in worker errors as a result.

Capital investment

A similar situation applies in terms of investment in capital – investment in new capital equipment is 40% higher per person in Germany than in the UK. As a result, German firms' equipment is on average more up to date, meaning that productivity is likely to be higher. Recent studies suggest that this lack of investment explains a substantial part of the UK's productivity gap, and the huge investment in IT and Internet technology in the US explains the major part of their productivity growth over the past decade.

Research and development

A third area in which investment is important is research and development, so that both products and processes can be improved. One problem in the UK is that firms have tended not to invest in this area – US firms invest 50% more as a percentage of **GDP** than UK firms. Improved processes lead to better use of time, so that more can be done with existing factor inputs.

Management techniques

Investment-related factors are not the only factors influencing productivity, nor are they necessarily the key ones. Management techniques and processes can have a major impact on productivity. A recent survey has shown a strong correlation between firms using modern management practices, such as teamwork and employee involvement, and productivity growth. By contrast, low-paying organisations, which are less likely to use such techniques, were shown to be less likely to experience productivity growth. This picture is complicated, however, by the fact that low-paying organisations are also less likely to invest in training and innovation. So, we see that it can be hard to isolate the impact of management techniques from other important factors influencing productivity.

Legislation

The final major factor affecting productivity is the legislative framework. Although the UK is comparatively free from legislative restrictions by European standards, there has been a trend towards greater regulation in recent years. Examples of recent legislation include the Working Time Directive, the 1999 Employee Relations Act and growing environmental protection legislation which requires more paperwork and lengthier procedures for disposing of manufacturing by-products. Nevertheless, given that the UK is less productive than other EU countries that already have comparable legislation in place, the impact of this legislation must be questioned – over the period 1980–1997 labour productivity in France, Germany and the UK grew at almost the same rate (about 30%).

Overall, the key factor affecting productivity is probably managerial outlook. Managerial outlook integrates most of they key factors identified above – the longer the view that the management take, the more likely they are to invest in people, processes and capital, and the more likely they are to use participative management techniques.

Unfortunately, management outlook can be difficult to change because of entrenched attitudes and positions, and also because managers may believe that they are being communicative when in fact they are not. In a workplace survey, 70% of managers felt that they consulted employees fully before any change. Unfortunately, only 30% of employees felt that their managers were good at providing them with the opportunity to comment. Similarly, whereas 90% of managers felt that employee relations were good, only 54% of employees came to the same conclusion. Therefore, raising productivity may mean more than simply changing management style; it is also about changing perceptions, a difficult hurdle to overcome.

PROGRESS CHECK

Explain two ways in which managers might increase a firm's productivity.

NUMERICAL INVESTIGATION

POSITION	PLANT	VEHICLES PER EMPLOYEE
1	Nissan (UK)	105
2	VW (Spain)	76
3	GM (Germany)	76
4	Fiat (Italy)	73
5	Toyota (UK)	72
6	SEAT (Spain)	69
7	Renault (France)	68
8	GM (Spain)	67
9	Renault (Spain)	64
10	Honda (UK)	64
11	Ford (UK)	59
13	Ford (Germany)	42
30=	Rover (UK)	30
30=	Mercedes (Germany)	30

Table 2.3 Productivity in the European car market
(Source: Economist Intelligence Unit)

1 Analyse possible reasons for the differences in productivity illustrated in the table.
2 Discuss the possible implications of the information in the table for European car manufacturers.

The government and productivity

The government can have both a positive and negative impact on productivity, in terms of its influence on the external environment of business.

Negative influence

Businesses increasingly complain about the burden of red tape and legislation that they have to deal with. They argue that this has become worse in recent years as a result of closer integration with the other EU States, which generally have more legislation designed to protect customers, employees and the environment.

Positive influence

In terms of its positive influence in this area, the government is trying to create a climate in which firms will want to invest more in people, capital, research and management techniques, and make better use of the inputs that they have got.

Competition

One way in which this can be encouraged is by creating more competition in markets. Over the last 20 years, more and more industries have been privatised and/or

deregulated. The increase in competition and exposure to market forces has had dramatic effects on productivity in some of these industries. At British Steel (formerly a nationalised industry), for example, it now takes a worker 3.3 hours to produce a tonne of liquid steel, compared to 14.3 hours in before it was privatised.

However, a potential danger with too much competition is that it can create short-term pressures which deter spending on training and new equipment.

Financial incentives

The Government has introduced a number of measures to stimulate spending in these areas. In the 1999 Budget, for example, a 10% corporation tax rate for small firms was announced to encourage enterprise and innovation, together with tax breaks on research and development, and investment in capital. In the run-up to the 2000 Budget, announcements were made about the reform of capital gains tax to improve incentives for entrepreneurial investment, a £40 million skills-raising package and incentives to increase employee share ownership.

The problem is judging how effective any of these measures will be. Governments have been concerned about low productivity in the UK for some time. The difficulty seems to be that there is a lack of understanding about exactly *why* firms in the UK invest less in people etc., than their international rivals. In the absence of such understanding, it is difficult to determine the most effective action for the government to take.

Obviously, the incentives created will have some effect. Putting more money into education and training will help to create a more skilled workforce. Investment grants should lead to more capital equipment being bought. However, how important these moves will be in influencing productivity is very difficult to judge, firstly because it will depend on how individual firms respond to the incentives created – e.g. how much new capital equipment will be bought – and secondly on how the new factors are used. An increased stock of high quality inputs is fine, but the impact on productivity depends on what firms do with them. The government can have little direct control over this, reducing its influence on productivity.

PROGRESS CHECK

What can a government do to to increase productivity?

Increasing productivity

The essence of increasing productivity is to increase spending on capital, labour, research, or management techniques, either to increase the quality of inputs or to make better use of them – capital productivity can be increased by increasing **capacity utilisation**, for example. However, to be effective, solutions need to be appropriate to the mix of factor inputs used.

The case of a major manufacturing plant in the US in the late 1980s serves as a warning. This firm spent 40% of its productivity budget on improving **direct labour** efficiency, but direct labour comprised only 10% of the firm's production costs. Soon after, the firm switched resources to making better use of its technology and its support staff.

Cutting jobs

One of the simplest steps for a firm seeking to improve labour productivity is to reduce the size of its workforce. The remaining employees then have to produce the same output by working harder, thereby increasing productivity. This input-minimising approach is rather a negative view though, and is likely to have long-term implications for labour turnover and quality. High labour turnover could well reduce productivity in the long term. Therefore, although simple, this method may not be particularly effective in the long term.

Motivational strategies

A more positive approach is to try to motivate employees to add more value, which should have positive outcomes for most stakeholders, through the success of the firm.

Generally improved motivation is likely to come through a more participative approach to management, and possibly through introducing performance-related pay. By tying individual payment levels to a productivity target, employees should be more motivated to achieve their goal. However, recent evidence on performance-related pay has been less encouraging: the Civil Service is abandoning its current system because of the damaging effect it has had on morale. Individuals were given targets at the start of each year and were then assessed on whether these were achieved. The problem is that most employees work as part of a team, and their individual contribution is difficult to isolate from that of the team as a whole. The damage to morale actually reduced productivity making the entire system counter-productive. Once again this suggests that, although simple in theory, raising productivity in practise may be quite difficult.

Information Technology (IT)

Some firms believe the answer to poor productivity lies in greater investment in IT. This should have the twin benefits of improving communication (and therefore making employees feel more involved) and having a direct effect on productivity by allowing tasks to be processed more quickly. However, although investment in this area has grown rapidly, the impact on productivity does not seem as clear cut as might have been hoped. Productivity growth in US manufacturing actually slowed down in the last 5 years of the twentieth century rather than increasing, in spite of a very high level of investment in computing and IT.

Training

Part of the reason for the disappointing effects of IT on productivity might be found in a recent study in the UK which uncovered that, in spite of the investment in IT, under 50% of employees in the survey had received training on communicating electronically, and three-quarters had received no training on dealing with information overload. A separate survey found that 75% of email messages are of no practical use, and up to half are deleted before they are even opened. This may suggest that productivity gains will be felt in the longer term, once people have adapted to new systems. However, some commentators wonder whether this will ever be the case given the continual innovation and change in the IT sector. Certainly, investment in IT without providing the training to go with it seems to be a recipe for disaster.

Investment

Other ways of improving productivity might include investing directly into capital and training. In the case of investment in capital, there may be an initial reduction in productivity as employees take time to adapt to the new technology. A good example is the well-documented troubles faced by the Passport Agency in the summer of 1999 following computerisation of the passport issuing system. The time taken to process an application rose from 10 days to 6 weeks, mainly due to staff being unfamiliar with the new system.

Training may give a quicker pay-off, but UK firms have invested less in training than international rivals, partly because of fear of poaching. Both the UK and US have very fluid labour markets, with employees changing jobs comparatively frequently. The problem for a firm is that, if an employee leaves, the firm loses the investment in training that it has made. It is tempting to 'poach' other firms' employees rather than training your own. This then leads to a skills shortage, in which organisations pay a premium for the few workers who do have the required skills.

The other point about training is that it does not necessarily improve productivity. While training is undertaken, productivity is likely to fall, and when complete, the results will depend on what type of training was undertaken in the first place. If the training is not specific to the job, it may be difficult to evaluate its impact.

The best approach

The best approach to productivity for an individual firm therefore depends on the circumstances. A highly capital-intensive firm would approach productivity very differently to a labour intensive firm. Whereas the latter would be looking at training and equiping employees, the capital-intensive firm would be more focused on keeping capacity utilisation high. Similarly, a service sector firm might find raising productivity more difficult than a manufacturing firm, because introducing more capital may not be an easy option.

To be successful most firms should focus on making the most of the labour and capital that they have and on developing these over time. To achieve this, a firm will need a flexible and motivated workforce, which in turn relies on an open and participative management approach. Once that is in place, it is likely that other pieces of the jigsaw (like effective training) will follow eventually. Without such an approach, the other policies by themselves are unlikely to have much effect – the

FACT FILE

Navistar, an engine producer in Indiana (US), has invested $285 million into capital improvements since 1995. Whereas in 1994 900 people produced 175 engines a day, in 2000 1900 workers produce 1400 engines per day – an increase in simple labour productivity of almost 300%.

employees may not feel included and may tend to resist change, meaning that money invested in new capital equipment or training is wasted.

It is clear that there are no simple solutions to a productivity problem – if it was straightforward to solve, there would not be a problem in the first place! Firms that have succeeded in raising productivity have been those that have involved their employees and been prepared to be patient – improvements require a fundamental change in approach throughout the organisation, and this is usually some time in coming.

PROGRESS CHECK

Explain the possible problems managers might face when trying to increase productivity.

Are improvements in productivity a good thing?

This might seem like a strange question. In principle increases in productivity make firms more competitive. This should generate rising profits, which can then be distributed between stakeholders as rising wages, lower prices and higher dividends to shareholders – rising productivity is often seen as a win-win proposition.

How great the all-round benefits of increasing productivity are will depend on how the improvements are brought about. If they are achieved through job cuts, then clearly the workforce as a whole is not benefiting. However, even if the firm improves productivity positively, through training and investment, there may still be a problem if demand for the firm's products does not increase. This is because rising productivity means that more units can be made with the same workforce – or the same number can be made with fewer workers. It is this fear of job losses that has led to conflict over productivity agreements in the past – the move towards multi-skilling, for example, has been resisted in many organisations, in the belief that flexible working cost jobs.

In the long term, however, improvements in productivity are needed for firms to survive, and employees and employers need to agree on how this can be achieved. If firms in other countries are becoming more and more productive, resistance to change will simply result in less productive firms becoming uncompetitive, at which point jobs will come under threat. A more positive way of looking at productivity is to say that improvements will lead firms to become more competitive, which should create its own demand, meaning that job losses are unnecessary. In theory at least.

FACT FILE

In exchange for agreeing changes in working practices, hoping to improve productivity, 160,000 Royal Mail workers received a 2% wage rise, a cut in their working week and improved pension benefits. The union and management claimed the agreement (made in February 2000) was a turning point in the service's history, and that the changes were necessary to compete in a deregulated environment. Both sides felt that they would benefit from the agreement.

FACT FILE

In November 1998 British Steel announced further job losses, in spite of dramatic productivity improvements over a 20 year period, using new mini-mill technology which requires only a fifth of the workforce needed for traditional methods. This is in spite of a reduction from a peak of 269,000 employees to under 50,000 today. At a meeting with Italian business people where he had discussed the job-loss program, the Personnel Director asked whether there were any questions. Someone asked. 'Do you take the same route home every night?' Source: *People Management* 12 November 1998

Approaching exam questions: productivity

How important is productivity in determining a firm's international competitiveness?

(11 marks)

This question is quite straightforward, provided the candidate focuses on 'how important'. Many candidates will overlook this, and give a one-sided account of why productivity is very important. Such an approach would gain very few evaluation marks. The give-away is in the number of marks available – any AS question with more than 10 marks will require an evaluative approach.

Some of the points that should be included are shown below.

Productivity is very important because:

■ It influences unit costs, which affect the price that can be charged.

■ High productivity may allow a firm to meet orders more quickly, giving the firm a competitive advantage.

■ An increase in productivity may allow the firm to make more profit per unit, which can be reinvested in product improvements, helping to make the firm more competitive in the long run.

But:

■ The market may not be price sensitive, so price cuts may be unimportant.

■ Other factors may be more important in determining international competitiveness, such as exchange rates or cultural differences.

■ Low productivity may be necessary for some firms to safeguard quality.

One way of ending would be to cite a couple of examples of firms, explaining why productivity would or would not be important in each case, and then to draw general conclusions from that.

Analyse the main obstacles a firm may face when trying to raise productivity.

(9 marks)

This is a standard sort of question, requiring the candidate to take an in-depth look at two or three key factors. There is no requirement to show judgement, just a logical train of argument.

Points to be analysed might include:

■ Resistance to change – productivity improvements generally require a change in patterns of working, and employees may fear that they will be unable to cope. This fear of the unknown is a major problem for firms attempting to introduce change.

■ Fear of job losses – a resistance to change is likely to be reinforced if employees think that job losses will occur once productivity improvements are made. If the firm can reassure workers (e.g. pointing to rising demand, giving guarantees etc.), this problem may be reduced.

■ Lack of funds – most productivity schemes require investment of some sort, so a shortage of funds can wreak havoc. Nevertheless, if productivity is a priority, most firms will be able to reallocate funds. Or borrow, although the latter course of action has well-known pitfalls.

■ Previous history – if a firm has a history of poor industrial relations, there may be a lack of trust and communication within the business, making it difficult to bring employees on board.

Which is more important for a firm – high quality or high productivity?

(11 marks)

The question here implies that there is an inevitable trade-off between productivity and quality, which a good candidate would notice. This provides a good opportunity for an evaluative conclusion – although productivity and quality are both important in different circumstances, there is no reason why they can't be achieved simultaneously.

Before embarking on a conclusion though, the question has to be answered directly. Relevant points might include:

■ Productivity might be more important in price elastic markets in which competition is strong, and there is little differentiation between products.

It might depend on the stage of the economic cycle. In recession, the firm might need to keep costs down and focus on low prices, making productivity more important.

■ What is the firm's target segment? A high income segment might make quality the key to success.

What do rival firms have – high quality or high productivity?

The key to a high mark is not to accept the trade-off; high quality and high productivity are often linked in a successful firm.

'The key determinant of productivity is a well-motivated workforce.' How true is this statement?

(11 marks)

Another evaluative question, with two clues this time – 'how true' and 'key determinant'. A weak answer would explain how a well-motivated workforce might improve productivity. A better one would look at other factors influencing productivity and would examine the circumstances in which motivation might be *the* most important factor.

Points that might be made include:

Motivation affects productivity, because a motivated employee is more likely to stay on at the end of the day to complete tasks etc. However, this does not make it the key factor.

The level of training provided by the firm might be more important than an enthusiastic approach in certain industries (e.g. where complex tasks need to be completed at speed).

■ Similarly, the level of capital investment might be important. A well-motivated employee cannot turn out many tonnes of steel without a blast furnace.

■ The importance of motivation in productivity might vary from sector to sector. Are there differences between service sector and manufacturing firms? Public and private sector?

The conclusion might be that motivation matters, but only when the other factors are present. Alternatively one might argue that, even if the other factors are present, unless the workforce is motivated, machinery and training will not be used effectively. The main thing is to come to a conclusion and justify it.

Summary chart

Figure 2.2 Productivity

Student answers

Discuss the factors that might determine a firm's productivity.

(11 marks)

Student answer

The main things that determine a firm's productivity are its workforce and its machines. If a firm has lots of workers and machines then its capacity utilisation will be high, which will make production high too. However, productivity depends on whether there is demand. If demand is low then productivity will be low too, since the firm will not be able to sell the goods, so it won't make them. In a capital-intensive industry, machinery will be the main factor in determining production, whereas in a labour-intensive industry, like strawberry picking, it will be the workforce that determines productivity.

Marker's comments

This answer is very weak, making a number of serious errors. Firstly, the candidate confuses productivity with production. Productivity is production per unit of input, but this candidate uses the terms interchangeably. In passing, the candidate also misunderstands capacity utilisation – more workers and machines do increase capacity, but not capacity utilisation, which is the percentage of capacity that is used.

On a good day, an examiner might see something worth a mark, but really there is nothing of any merit.

Mark: Content 0/2, Application & Analysis 0/6, Evaluation 0/3. Total = 0

Analyse reasons why a firm might decide not to try to increase its productivity.

(9 marks)

Student answer

The most obvious reason for not wanting to increase productivity is if there is no need. Suppose the firm was already 20% more productive than the next best firm in its market. It will already have lower costs per unit (since each worker and machine will be making more units per day) and can, therefore, under-cut its rival. A further increase in productivity might increase the advantage further, but since increasing productivity usually costs money (upgrading machinery or doing more training), the firm might be better advised to use the money elsewhere.

The firm might do better to invest in new product development, giving it a new angle to attack competitors from. Being the most productive firm does not mean people necessarily want to buy what you make. So, if the firm is worried that its product is nearing the end of its life cycle, R&D might be a better use of funds than increasing productivity further.

Marker's comments

This is a strong answer, which shows that it is not necessary to make lots of different points to get a high mark. This answer takes one basic idea and explores it to its logical extent. What is particularly impressive is that every point is justified with an example or explanation, leaving the examiner in no doubt that the candidate understands fully what they are saying. There are other points that could have been made, but this candidate made sure of getting analysis marks by developing their main point fully.

Mark: Content 2/2, Application 3/3, Analysis 4/5. Total = 9

To what extent can government policy determine a UK firm's labour productivity.

(11 marks)

Student answer

The government can have a big impact on a firm's productivity through the laws that it passes. The recent European Working Time Directive, for example, restricts the working week to 48 hours. In some industries where long hours are normal, like truck driving, this means that the firms will have to employ more workers to get the same amount of work done, which will reduce labour productivity.

On the other hand, the government has announced that in the next Budget, there will be more grants towards training and education (£10 million package to improve enterprise skills in schools). This means that firms will have better skilled workers in the future, because enterprise skills must include some knowledge of business. Therefore, workers will take less time to settle in, making productivity higher.

In conclusion, the government is a major determinant of UK firm's productivity.

Marker's comments

This candidate is very well informed about the business world, and has produced a good answer. There is good application to the question, focusing strongly on both government policy and productivity. In fact, the focus on policy is the answer's Achilles heel – the answer does not evaluate by looking at why government policy might not make any real difference. Nevertheless, the answer exhibits strong analysis, and would therefore score relatively well.

Mark: Content 2/2, Application & Analysis 5/6, Evaluation 0/3. Total = 7

To what extent are improvements in productivity likely to benefit a firm's workforce?

(11 marks)

Student answer

The most obvious way in which an increase in productivity (assuming the question means labour productivity) would benefit the workforce is if the workers are on some sort of performance-related or piece-rate pay. In that case, if each worker is making more units per hour, then they will be paid more; a clear benefit.

However, this is an over-simplification. Whether an increase in productivity actually benefits the workforce in the long run will depend on the process through which the 'improvement' is introduced. For example, if the firm tries to increase productivity through a program of job cuts, employees will not benefit. If, however, the firm invests in training, workers will benefit through an increase in their employability, especially if the skills gained are transferable.

Another factor influencing the impact on employees will be the state of the external environment. If demand is rising due to economic growth, productivity increases will lead to increased sales, meaning that jobs are secure. If a firm is in a declining market (like British Steel in the 1980s), productivity gains may simply result in more job losses – there might not be the demand for an increased output. On the other hand, without gains in productivity, the firm might become so uncompetitive (due to high unit costs) that it is forced out of business, meaning that all jobs would be lost.

Marker's comments

A very high quality, thoughtful answer which uses very businesslike language, giving the answer an evaluative feel. Although the answer does not come to a conclusion about the 'extent', the candidate does use an evaluative approach throughout – 'it depends on x because of y' – and as a result would receive evaluation marks. The analysis is strong, tracing through arguments to their logical conclusion, and the answer is well focused on the question.

Mark: Content 2/2, Application & Analysis 6/6, Evaluation 2/3. Total = 10

End of section questions

1 Benson plc makes extractor fans. Its labour productivity is 25% higher than any other firm in the market. Consider how Benson might respond to this situation.

(11 marks)

2 Analyse the possible circumstances in which productivity improvements might be vital to a firm's survival.

(9 marks)

3 To what extent is there a trade-off between productivity and quality?

(11 marks)

4 To what extent is it easier to raise productivity in a manufacturing firm than in the service sector?

(11 marks)

5 Outline the main problems a firm is likely to face when seeking to raise productivity.

(9 marks)

6 How important is it for a firm to increase its productivity?

(9 marks)

7 Consider the possible reasons that UK firms on average spend less per worker on training than firms in mainland Europe.

(11 marks)

8 Discuss the factors that might make a firm's attempt to increase productivity more likely to succeed.

(11 marks)

9 TRL Ltd has labour productivity which is 20% lower than its main rival. Discuss the factors that might determine how TRL should respond to this situation.

(11 marks)

10 Discuss the extent to which a well-motivated workforce is likely to have a high level of productivity.

(11 marks)

Essays

1 'US firms are more productive because they have fewer regulations governing them. Therefore, the UK government should aim to cut back on legislation, such as employment protection, to give UK firms a level playing field.' To what extent do you agree with this statement?

(40 marks)

2 'Productivity improvements will lead inevitably to redundancies, and should be resisted by employees.' Discuss.

(40 marks)

3 'Unproductive firms are doomed to failure.' Discuss.

(40 marks)

4 'Innovation is more significant than productivity in today's marketplace'. To what extent do you agree with this statement?

(40 marks)

5 Although UK firms are on average 20% less productive than those in France and Germany, UK exports have grown by an average 6% a year since 1994. Discuss the factors which might explain this apparent paradox.

(40 marks)

CHAPTER 3

Scale of production

Introduction

The choice of an appropriate **scale** of production for a firm is one that involves two interrelated concepts; those of **economies** (and **diseconomies**) **of scale** on the one hand, and **capacity utilisation** on the other.

An economist would say that all factors of production have to be increased for scale economies to be derived. So, economies of scale arise when the firm, for example, moves to larger premises, with more employees and more capital equipment.

In principle, the firm should be able to drive down its unit costs because of its larger size. A larger firm can afford to employ managerial specialists, such as a Human Resources department, allowing the firm to get the best out of its employees, helping to drive down labour turnover, and freeing up management time to concentrate on key issues. A larger organisation can also put pressure on suppliers to lower their prices. In addition, there are associated technical advantages to be gained from using specialist equipment and production techniques, such as labour specialisation.

However, such advantages can only be exploited if the firm is able to fully utilise its larger scale. Hence capacity utilisation is also significant in this context. There are unlikely to be many benefits to be derived from a larger scale unless demand increases proportionately. If demand does not increase, the firm will simply have incurred expenses for little gain, with its new factory space operating at half power.

When deciding on an appropriate scale of production managers must take into account the benefits that can be derived from scale economies, as well as appreciating both the need to keep capacity utilisation high and to allow for future growth.

KEY TERMS

Economies of scale
are cost advantages that result from a move to a larger scale of production

Capacity utilisation
measures the existing output in relation to the maximum possible output. Firms which produce more with existing resources are increasing their capacity utilisation.
An increase in **scale** means an increase in the firm's capacity.

PROGRESS CHECK

What is the difference between an increase in scale and an increase in capacity utilisation?

The number of units a firm decides to produce will not just depend on unit cost; it will also depend on demand.

Economies of scale and growth

Specialisation and mass production

Traditionally, economies of scale derive from specialisation and mass production – it was the economies of scale that enabled Henry Ford to produce the model T at an affordable price. Ford took advantage of large-scale production to divide the production process into simple tasks, which employees were trained to carry out very fast. Ford also generated the sales volume to be able to mechanise, allowing production to take place even faster and reducing the unit costs of production further.

KEY POINTS

A firm is most likely to benefit from economies of scale if:

- large scale production allows more efficient production techniques
- there are significant discounts from bulk purchasing
- specialisation of labour is possible
- it is possible to borrow more cheaply with more assets.

NUMERICAL INVESTIGATION

	FORD	TOTAL US PRODUCTION (000s)
1903	1.7	11.2
1904	1.7	22.1
1905	1.6	24.2
1906	8.7	33.2
1907	14.9	43.0
1908	10.2	63.5
1909	17.8	123.9
1910	32.1	181.0
1911	69.8	199.3
1912	170.2	356.0
1913	202.7	461.5
1914	308.2	548.1
1915	501.5	895.1
1916	734.8	1525.5
1917	622.4	1745.7
1919	820.4	1651.6
1920	419.5	1905.5
1921	903.8	1468.0
1922	1173.7	2274.1
1923	1817.9	3624.7

Table 3.1 United States passenger car output (Source: US Department of Commerce; Nevins and Hill, *Ford: decline and rebirth 1933–1962*)

1 Calculate Ford's output as a percentage of total US production in 1903 and 1923.
2 Calculate the increase in Ford production from 1903 to 1923.
3 Analyse the possible reasons why this growth was so rapid.

FACT FILE

A good recent example of technical economies of scale is Boeing's announcement that it is to spend $3 billion on either a 550-seat version of its 747 plane or a new and even larger jet (possibly 800 seats). The advantage of carrying more passengers per plane is a classic economies of scale.

Supply chain management

Another area in which cost savings can be made is in **supply chain management**. A large organisation can reduce costs substantially by putting pressure on its suppliers to hold down prices. General Electric, the giant US conglomerate, is infamous for using its combined buying power to force down suppliers' margins to minimal levels. Some commentators suggest that there is a limit to how far margins can be driven down – if a firm buys 20 million units from suppliers with low margins, how much difference would an order of 40 million units make? Benefits would be gained only if the suppliers were able to make cost savings from the bigger order, which might not be technically possible, as previously noted.

Internal growth

Other possible areas where economies of scale can be achieved through **internal growth** include financial and mangerial economies. Larger firms may be able to borrow more cheaply because they have more collateral; they may also be able to employ specialist managers.

External growth

Economies of scale may also be achieved through **external growth** and are believed to be a major motive behind mergers and take-overs. An article in *The Guardian* newspaper, referring to the recent wave of merger and take-over activity, suggested only half jokingly that 'it surely cannot be long before the world's big companies recognise the logic of "synergistic rationalisation" and fuse together to form a single corporation'.

Although obviously far-fetched, *The Guardian* was commenting on the fact that the value of mergers and acquisitions in Europe in 1998 broke all records, and then proceeded to double in 1999. In most cases the rationale behind this activity was at least partly due to the quest for economies of scale.

In particular, mergers and take-overs seem to be driven by the opportunity for managerial and research economies. In the former case, functions such as Human Resources and Information Technology support can be slimmed down – there is no need, for example, to have two Human Resource Directors. Middle managers are also a target in such mergers, because within the different organisations there are usually people doing essentially the same job – in the merged organisation, for example, there is only a need for one economic forecast whereas in the pre-merged companies, each firm would have needed one.

There are similar savings to be made in research – often pre-merged companies are researching the same technologies in similar ways, and such projects can be combined. The result should be that the two organisations continue to be as effective as before, but with fewer people because of overlap between the two businesses (termed '**synergistic rationalisation**').

It is these gains from reducing overlap – the cost savings that can be reaped as a result of rationalisation – that seem to be driving a number of mergers. The numbers are clear – the merger of CGU and Norwich Union in February 2000 was forecast (by CGU's Chief Executive) to cut £200 million a year from their combined costs; a significant scale economy.

Disadvantages of merger

Research by economists over the years has suggested that, in the majority of cases, the merged organisation performs less well than the organisations would have done separately. Obviously, such research is fraught with difficulty, because nobody can know for sure what would have happened to the two original companies, but it does point to a need for caution when discussing the benefits that can be derived from larger scales.

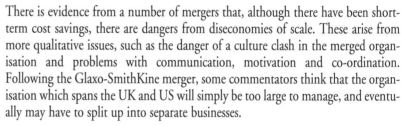

PROGRESS CHECK

What sorts of scale economy are most likely to be available to a service sector organisation, such as a chain of travel agents?

Diseconomies of scale

There is evidence from a number of mergers that, although there have been short-term cost savings, there are dangers from diseconomies of scale. These arise from more qualitative issues, such as the danger of a culture clash in the merged organisation and problems with communication, motivation and co-ordination. Following the Glaxo-SmithKine merger, some commentators think that the organisation which spans the UK and US will simply be too large to manage, and eventually may have to split up into separate businesses.

Diseconomies of scale are difficult to quantify and, therefore, may not be taken properly into account when decisions on scale are made. Consequently, there may be a tendency to overemphasise the visible savings to be made from a larger business and to underemphasise the organisational difficulties that may result.

In some ways the significance of economies of scale may actually lie in the fact that they are *perceived to be important*, and it is this perception that is helping to drive the current wave of mergers forwards. The perception of the concept may, therefore, have more significance than the concept itself.

It is also important to remember that, in spite of the trend towards large organisations, there are many successful comparatively small firms in existence – some serve small markets, such as Porsche in the car industry. Others, such as Honda, compete by using their smaller size to be more responsive to changing customer needs. Therefore, although economies of scale are clearly significant, there are many profitable firms which continue to exist without seeming to take full advantage of the scale economies available.

KEY POINTS

Economies of scale may be more significant:

- in industries where R&D is important
- during mergers of culturally similar organisations
- in manufacturing organisations.

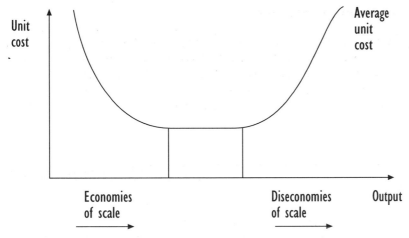

Figure 3.1 Economies and diseconomies of scale

Are diseconomies of scale inevitable?

Diseconomies of scale come about, in principle, because of the managerial difficulties inherent in running a larger organisation.

In theory, it becomes more difficult to communicate effectively with a larger workforce – the number of levels of hierarchy in the organisation may begins to rise, and senior managers may become detached from the day-to-day running of the business. Also, if the number of levels of hierarchy is allowed to rise, communications will tend to slow down, both vertically and laterally, making the organisation less adaptable to change.

Additionally, as a business becomes spread over a number of sites and countries, it tends to become much harder to co-ordinate activities, and to make sure that the different parts of the organisation are pulling in the same direction.

Finally, it is argued, it becomes more difficult to motivate employees in large organisations, because they do not feel important. According to these arguments, there should be a size beyond which organisations become vulnerable and uncompetitive.

In spite of apparent diseconomies of scale there has been an ongoing rise in the average size of organisations over the last 30 years, and these organisations have managed to remain profitable in the face of a changing competitive environment, which suggests that, although it is possible that diseconomies of scale could arise in a growing organisation, it is not inevitable. Or at least that the diseconomies do not outweigh the economies.

FACT FILE

A recent study in the US estimates that there are substantial diseconomies of scale in large hospitals, finding, for example, that the typical patient will be asked their name an average of 42 times during a hospital stay.

PROGRESS CHECK

How large do you think a school can become before diseconomies of scale would set in? What form might these diseconomies take?

Managing to prevent diseconomies of scale

Essentially, diseconomies of scale are managerial in nature (relating to communication, co-ordination, and motivation), which should mean that effective management techniques can be devised to help overcome them (management techniques are covered in the *People Management* title in this series). In recent years, organisations have **delayered** and **decentralised** to overcome the communications difficulties inherent in tall organisational structures. **Empowerment** of employees has become more widespread, helping to tackle problems with motivation by making employees feel more 'included'. **Management by Objectives** is a management technique specifically designed to help co-ordinate the different parts of large and diverse organisations.

For example, in February 2000, Philips announced that it was to split its consumer electronics division into five separate units in an attempt to improve 'cost transparency'. The new structure was designed to allow the businesses to react more quickly to changing market conditions. The implication of this is that Philips felt that it was suffering from managerial diseconomies, increasing costs and reducing responsiveness. It has responded by redesigning its management structure to get round these problems and, hopefully, will eliminate these diseconomies.

So, diseconomies of scale are not inevitable, especially if the organisation has grown organically, meaning that preventative management techniques can be introduced gradually as the need arises. In addition, the recent growth of the use of IT facilities, such as intranets, has made the task of communicating between diverse parts of large organisations easier. Perhaps diseconomies of scale will be less of a problem in the future, although recent reports suggest that communicating through IT is actually making communications problems worse because of the volume of semi-relevant, or irrelevant, information that is being sent, resulting in information overload.

In conclusion, there is significant evidence that diseconomies of scale *do* exist in many organisations. A study has found that return on equity for the 10 largest US banks was 15.5%, whereas for the next 10 largest it was 17.2%, suggesting that diseconomies of scale exist for the largest banks. Although it may be possible to avoid diseconomies of scale in principle, the reality may be somewhat different. However, the other advantages of large scale, such as reduced risk of take-over, are likely to mean that the drive towards large scale will continue, in spite of the possibility of some cost disadvantages.

KEY POINTS

Diseconomies of scale are more likely in organisations:

- that are geographically spread
- without a clear mission
- with a tall hierarchy and small span of control
- that use an authoritarian management style
- which fail to prepare for growth
- which have experienced rapid growth
- which have poor management.

PROGRESS CHECK

To what extent can diseconomies of scale be avoided?

Benefits of an increase in scale

An increase in scale ought to work to the benefit of an organisation – it will tend to have more power in the market, and should be able to take advantage of economies of scale. However, these economies of scale will not come about automatically – an increase in scale by itself is not a particular advantage to the firm – what matters is how the firm *uses* the increase in scale.

For example, a larger firm may have the ability to put pressure on suppliers, but only if it does so actively and in the right way. Therefore, a firm with better negotiating skills will tend to derive more benefit from an increase in scale than a firm with weak ones. Similarly, an increase in scale does not give the firm specialisation advantages – these will only come about if the firm redesigns its production process to maximise the advantages of a larger scale operation.

Another key point is the state of the market. Whilst an increase in scale might be able to generate some demand in its own right (lower unit costs might allow the firm to charge lower prices), unless demand is generally on an upward trend, the firm might find it difficult to make the most of its increase in size. Certainly in the short term, capacity utilisation is likely to fall as a result of an increase in scale, and this might cancel out any benefits derived from economies of scale.

The importance of planning

The benefits that a firm experiences from an increase in scale will depend on the skills of the management team, and the amount of planning and consultation that takes place. This is important because an increase in the scale of operations is likely to mean a change in working patterns for most employees. Unless they feel involved in the process, they may feel alienated, which is likely to reduce the potential benefits.

An unplanned expansion is likely to run into trouble. This is because lack of planning is likely to mean that new communications systems have not been thought through, which will probably make co-ordination of the different parts of the larger firm more difficult. New employees hired as part of the expansion may not feel part of the organisation, leading to motivation problems. These features are the classic hallmarks of diseconomies of scale.

This analysis may go some way to explaining the poor performance of some merged organisations. By the very nature of such deals, advance planning is very difficult, so it is unsurprising that many merged firms have tended to struggle. The lure of short-term cost savings from merging support functions seems to outweigh the need for careful planning in many cases, although there are obvious counterexamples – Microsoft, for example, has grown to its current size partly through an aggressive acquisition policy.

Is there an 'optimal' scale of operation?

In theory, the optimal scale of production is the plant size that minimises unit costs. This obviously varies from industry to industry – the optimal scale of operation for a vehicle manufacturer is very different to that of a flower shop. Car plants tend to

be large, employing several thousand workers; supermarket outlets medium sized, employing dozens of workers; flower shops small, employing a handful of workers.

A more relevant question to ask is what is the optimal scale for a particular organisation as a whole? Even here, we must define what is meant by 'optimal'. Many business managers prefer their firms to stay at a small scale, because they are easy to manage, and provide a safe, satisfactory income for the owners. In such cases, a very small scale may be optimal, even if it is not the scale that minimises unit costs or maximises profit.

In theory, however, it should be possible to determine an 'optimal' scale of operations because there comes a point where further expansion of the organisation becomes uneconomic, either due to diseconomies of scale or the constraints of the marketplace. For many firms the marketplace seems to have been the significant restraining factor. Although diseconomies of scale may exist, they seem to be outweighed by the desire for safety in the form of high market share.

> **The best size for a firm to be depends on its owners' objectives, its managers' skills, market demand and unit costs.**

Scale and the market

In many industries, the main constraint on scale has been the marketplace. If a firm has exhausted its home market and entered new ones, these new markets may demand different products, therefore failing to deliver economies of scale and putting a brake on further expansion.

The global market

In a number of markets it seems that the old rules no longer apply, as a result of globalisation. The increasing harmonisation of laws (such as within the EU) allows firms to develop products in different trading blocs. This means that firms have to have effective distribution networks in many countries, which is accelerating the trend towards globalisation. Whereas in the past, a national firm was the optimal scale in many markets, today an international or even global scale may be optimal.

The Glaxo-SmithKline merger is an example of a company operating on a global scale. Following the harmonisation of patent processes in the EU and US in 1997, there is now a single market in pharmaceuticals. Therefore, the optimal scale has increased – there are economies of scale to be derived from a transatlantic conglomerate, because the need to develop drugs in two separate markets has disappeared, creating a strong motivation for the merger.

So, it is difficult to say what the optimal scale is for a firm in any industry, or even whether there is one at all. Increasing globalisation is creating firms that are larger than was thought economic in the past. Perhaps we have reached a point where there is no longer any economic constraint on the optimal size of firm. Will the only constraints be externally imposed, by legislators, who fear the power of global corporations? The recent US court case which threatens to break up Microsoft into smaller competing parts could be an example.

Is it always better for firms to be bigger rather than smaller?

Are economies of scale necessary for a firm to survive?

Looking at the current structure of UK industry, the answer to this question is clearly no. In the UK, 95% of businesses have fewer than 10 employees. There are many examples of firms which are successful even though they do *not* attempt to generate economies of scale. For example, they may serve niche markets, or have customers who are prepared to pay higher prices for the perceived higher quality or associated status of a non-mass produced product or service.

Examples of this type of firm include Fired Earth, the reproduction paint company which competes with mainstream paint producer Crown-Berger; sports car manufacturers Morgan and TVR which compete in the European car market; Dan computers which competes with Dell and Compaq. However, some analysts think that even producers in quite small niches may come under threat as flexible manufacturing systems develop further and allow large-scale operations to produce individually tailored products. For example, Ford has developed three radically different cars, the Jaguar S type, the Ford Thunderbird and a Lincoln sedan, all using the same basic chassis.

NUMERICAL INVESTIGATION

NUMBER OF EMPLOYEES	NUMBER OF MANUFACTURING UNITS		
	1989	1998	% CHANGE
1–9	107,155	126,170	+17.7
10–19	17,250	22,690	+31.5
20–49	17,519	16,350	−6.7
50–99	7708	6755	−12.4
100–199	4920	2810	−8.3
200–499	3323	2810	−15.4
500–999	930	690	−25.8
1000+	433	255	−41.1
TOTAL	**159,238**	**180,255**	**+13.2**

Table 3.2 The size of businesses measured by the number of employees per manufacturing unit (Source: *Annual Abstract of Statistics* 1999)

1 What percentage of manufacturing units have less than 10 employees?
2 How else might you measure the size of a business?
3 Analyse the possible reasons for the growth in the number of manufacturing units with less than 10 employees.

So, the picture that seems to be emerging is a future in which firms are either tiny niche players or giant super-sellers. The question is, therefore, whether there is room for medium-sized independent players in the global marketplace? One firm that offers hope for such a scenario is Honda, which has resolutely refused to consider teaming up with any other car producers, despite the avalanche of mergers over the last couple of years.

NUMERICAL INVESTIGATION

	Vehicle sales (millions)	Profit ($BN)	Turnover ($BN)
GM	8.1	2.9	161
DaimlerChrysler	4.5	5.6	15
Ford	6.8	5.9	143
Toyota	4.7	3.0	106
Renault/Nissan	4.9	1.2	95
VW	4.8	1.2	71
Honda	2.3	2.5	52

Table 3.3 Car sales, turnover and profitability (Scource: *Business Week* 5 July 1999)

1 Calculate Honda's output as a percentage of GM's.
2 Calculate profit as a percentage of turnover for all the companies above.
3 Comment on your findings.
4 Calculate the profit per vehicle for each of the producers above.

How does Honda survive?

In spite of Honda's comparatively small scale (less than half the volume of its next biggest rival), its profitability compares favourably with many of the other firms listed. In theory, Honda ought to be suffering due to lack of economies of scale, but this seems not to be the case.

Honda's advantage seems to lie in its cost-efficient, flexible manufacturing systems, allowing it to respond to changing consumer tastes much faster than its rivals – Honda is investing $1 billion in updating its already efficient plants in all its main markets, to keep ahead of its rivals. In Japan, Honda can already make as many as eight different models on one production line, and Honda's vision of the future is designing production lines that can change instantly from producing one model to another.

Honda wants to be the fastest to respond to changing consumer tastes – by being the first to respond to new trends, they can sell products at a price premium, making them less dependent on scale economies. An example is the Odyssey mini-van launched in late 1998 in the US which is winning sales from Chrysler and Ford's competing models, even though the Odyssey is $2000–4000 more expensive.

Therefore, it does seem likely that determined firms will be able to succeed, even if they do not benefit from the same economies of scale as their larger rivals by using their smaller size to respond more quickly to changing consumer tastes. The likely

°NUMERICAL INVESTIGATION

Number of buses needed on the road at peak times	Annual operating costs ($000)	Vehicle hours	Passenger miles (000s)	Cost per vehicle hour	Cost per passenger mile
1000+	3,117	39,646	5,071	$78.61	$0.615
500–999	2,070	30,462	3,694	$67.94	$0.56
250–499	1,422	21,771	2,995	$65.33	$0.475
100–249	1,340	24,283	3,216	$55.18	$0.417
50–99	405	7840	806	$51.68	$0.503
25–49	373	7885	746	$47.29	$0.5
1–24	306	5950	465	$51.35	$0.656

Table 3.4 An analysis of the US public transport bus system, 1995

1 What does the table suggest about economies and diseconomies of scale in the US public transport system?
2 Analyse the factors that might explain this pattern.

problem is that because of their smaller scale, they are less likely to be able to survive a severe marketing setback – large scale does not just mean lower unit costs, it also means more resources to draw on in an emergency.

PROGRESS CHECK

Can small firms survive in markets where there are significant economies of scale?

Capacity utilisation

High capacity utilisation means that the firm's production levels are close to their maximum. The main advantage of this is that the firm's fixed costs will be spread over a large number of units. This is particularly important in industries where fixed costs are very high, such as heavy manufacturing (steel and vehicles, etc.) and research-based markets like pharmaceuticals.

The high level of fixed costs means that the **break-even output** in such markets is high. Therefore, if firms cannot sell large numbers of units, they operate at a loss. This has led, at times, to savage competition between firms. The world car market, where it is estimated there is up to 30% overcapacity, is a classic example at the present time, with serious price cutting in Europe and a large number of mergers aimed at cutting spare capacity, thereby reducing fixed costs.

In markets where fixed costs are lower, capacity utilisation may be less important – in some markets with seasonal demand, firms deliberately build in excess capacity

KEY TERM

The breakeven output is the number of units at which all the costs are covered but no profit is made.

FACT FILE

In the summer months, Blackpool Pleasure Beach attracts millions of visitors, sometimes creating long queues. In the winter, it shuts down completely, therefore alternating between capacity utilisation of 100 and 0%.

to allow them to deal with seasonal surges. For large parts of the year, these firms will have very low capacity utilisation.

Similarly, in markets with limited competition, firms may be less concerned about utilising their capacity to its fullest extent. Such firms will probably be able to pass their higher costs onto the consumer, and might find the spare capacity a useful deterrent to potential competitors – competitors might fear that the incumbent firms could drive up output very quickly and cut prices before the new firms had got a foothold in the market. Where there is more competition though, firms want to avoid low capacity utilisation, because it produces higher fixed costs leading to cost disadvantages.

KEY POINTS

A high level of capacity utilisation is more important:

- where fixed costs are high
- in a competitive marketplace
- where demand is stable over time
- when profit margins are relatively small.

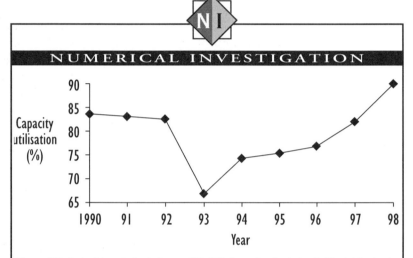

NUMERICAL INVESTIGATION

Figure 3.2 Road vehicle production in Germany 1990–1998 (Source: Deutsches Institut für Wirtschaftsforschung) Analyse the factors that might account for the changes in capacity utilisation shown in the chart.

Increasing capacity utilisation

If a firm's capacity utilisation is low, there must be a reason and this should provide the key to the best way to increase it. If for example, the economy is in recession, and all firms are facing a situation of excess capacity then, provided the firm is still profitable, there may not be a need to do anything. When the economy recovers demand should rise, increasing utilisation. Similarly, seasonal firms may accept low levels of capacity utilisation at certain times of the year as an inevitable consequence of operating in their particular market (although some firms get round this problem by producing a range of products with sales that peak at different times of the year).

If there is no obvious external reason for low capacity utilisation though, action may need to be taken. Most firms would like to increase its capacity utilisation by increasing sales – the firm gets the maximum benefit from its own capacity. In the short run, however, such an increase in utilisation might be difficult to achieve – there must be a reason why people are not buying the firm's products.

An important first step is therefore to analyse the situation: what is the current utilisation and what level of utilisation is plausible in future? If the firm estimates that it is unlikely to get near 100% utilisation before its equipment becomes obsolete, a program of rationalisation may be best. The firm would sell off excess capacity for the best price. Obviously, if the firm estimates that this capacity is likely to be needed in the near future, this option is less appealing.

An alternative short-term solution is to look for sub-contracting work – a number of leading paint producers also produce own brand products for retailers like B&Q. The Bourneville factory, as well as making chocolate for Cadbury, has also made Marks and Spencers' own version of KitKat. As well as generating revenue, this helps to spread fixed costs, although there is always a danger that the firm may sacrifice sales of its own main product.

In conclusion, much depends on the cause of low capacity utilisation in the first place. If the cause is external and short term, there may be little that the firm could or even should do. If the problem is longer term, action probably should be taken, but what is most appropriate will depend entirely on the firm's analysis of its situation.

PROGRESS CHECK

World-wide integrated circuit fabrication capacity rose to 1.796 million units a week in the fourth quarter of 1999, up from 1.754 million in the third quarter. Capacity utilisation is also up to 93.6%, from 90.8% in the third quarter.

Questions

1 Calculate total world-wide production in the third and fourth quarters of 1999.
2 Analyse possible reasons for the simultaneous increase in both capacity and capacity utilisation in the integrated circuit market.

Is high capacity utilisation a good thing?

Generally, high capacity utilisation is considered to be a good thing, because it indicates that productivity is high, keeping down unit costs – the firm is making effective use of its capital assets.

However, as capacity utilisation approaches (or exceeds through overtime working) 100%, the firm's resources may start to become overstretched. This can have a number of implications:

■ If there is a problem with production, there is no alternative capacity that can be brought on line. Consequently, there is a danger of missing delivery dates, damaging the firm's reputation.

■ When the firm is working flat out, there is a danger of defects occurring because of the pressure – employees may feel less able to stop the production line when they see a fault. Again, this may dent the firm's reputation.

■ The firm may be less able to respond to a sudden surge in demand. If there was spare capacity, the firm could bring this on-line, and meet new orders quickly. If capacity utilisation is close to 100%, then orders may be lost to the firm's competitors.

So, there is a difficult balance to be struck between productivity and flexibility. This balance can be easier to manage if the firm can work on reducing the lead time between order and delivery. If the firm can decrease this significantly, then even if problems do occur, the firm should still be able to deliver within an acceptable time frame.

PROGRESS CHECK

Questions

1 In December 1998, Samsung India Electronics, a manufacturer of televisions and a subsidiary of the South Korean firm Samsung, announced its intention to raise capacity utilisation from 70% to 100% in the next three months. The aim was to increase production to 2000 sets a day early in 1999, from its 1998 average of 1500 sets.

   Discuss the possible problems Samsung India Electronics might face in increasing its capacity utilisation.

2 Discuss the ways in which a firm might react if it is experiencing under utilisation of capacity.

Approaching exam questions: scale of production

Discuss whether greater flexibility or lower costs is more important for a firm in today's marketplace

(11 marks)

In essence this is a fairly straightforward question, and a good candidate would explain why each of these might be important in different markets, and would then explain the circumstances under which each might be *more* important than the other. Such an answer would score well, focusing properly on the question. A really high quality answer would challenge the assumption that low cost and flexibility cannot be achieved simultaneously, and would explain circumstances in which the two could be achieved together.

Relevant factors might include:

- Flexibility is more important in dynamic, growing environments.

  Lower cost might be more important in stable but competitive markets.

  Lower cost might be important in price elastic markets with a high degree of price competition.

- Flexibility is more important where demand is volatile, or where tastes can change rapidly

  But both flexibility and low cost might be possible given the move towards flexible manufacturing systems.

Discuss the factors which might determine the optimum size for a firm.

(11 marks)

This question requires the candidate to look in detail at a number of factors that influence size, but a high grade is unlikely to be gained unless the candidate deals with '*the optimum*'. This phrase is highly ambiguous, because it does not say optimum in terms of what. The natural temptation would be to assume that optimum means lowest cost, but adopting this approach would probably mean sacrificing any evaluation marks.

A good answer would start off by examining what optimum might mean – lowest cost? Highest profit? Most satisfaction for the owner? And would then use this as the basis for discussion.

Relevant points might include:

- potential for scale economies (in manufacturing this is generally greater, so the optimum size might be greater)

- current level of capacity utilisation

■ managerial skills present in the firm

■ state of demand in the market

■ objectives of the owner.

Assuming that the answer deals with 'optimum' early on, then the conclusion is straightforward: 'If optimum is taken to mean x, then y would be the key factor, because ... whereas if optimum means a then b would be the key factor, because ...

Done well, this should gain all the evaluation marks available on this type of question.

Discuss how important economies of scale are likely to be in determining a manufacturing firm's international competitiveness.

(11 marks)

The danger with this sort of question is that the candidate will fix on the phrase 'economies of scale', and then write everything that they know. Whilst such an approach would score one or two marks for knowledge, it simply wouldn't address what is, in fact, quite a complex question.

To score well on this question, an answer would need to focus on the phrases 'how important', 'manufacturing firm' and 'international competitiveness'; not an easy task. A good approach would be to assess why economies of scale might be more important in determining manufacturing competitiveness compared to service competitiveness (or not, as the case may be), and then to go on to analyse why economies of scale won't be the only factor.

Relevant points might include:

■ There is more scope for technical economies in manufacturing than in services.

■ Manufacturing is generally more competitive in international markets (it is difficult to export many services).

■ Nevertheless, some service sector firms have seen a great deal of merger activity, driven by globalisation and the need for economies of scale.

■ But many other factors which will affect competitiveness – quality, exchange rates, tastes etc.

One way to conclude would be to summarise one situation in which economies of scale will be really important, and one where they will not matter, and then use that to state some general principles, which should be supported by the main body of analysis.

Analyse why a firm might prefer not to increase its scale of operations.

(9 marks)

This is a straightforward question in which the candidate is invited to look in depth at the issue of scale. The obvious pitfall is to overlook the word 'not', and to write about economies of scale. Once this has been negotiated, the main thing is to limit the number of issues explored. Only 2 out of 9 marks are for knowledge, so only 2 or 3 different points are needed to get full marks, provided there is depth of analysis.

To achieve the required depth, the answer would have to take a factor like the owner's objectives, explain why these might mean that an increase in scale is not advisable, and then carry the answer one step further, perhaps by looking at what might happen if the scale of operations did increase.

Relevant points might include:

■ current capacity utilisation – perhaps there is no need for an increase in scale

■ state of demand and other external factors

■ objectives of the owners

■ skills and procedures available to deal with a larger scale

■ fear of moving out of local or national markets.

The temptation to run through all of these in detail should be avoided, however. Two or three of these explained in full would be sufficient to score a top mark on this question.

Student answers

Discuss how a small firm might aim to compete with a larger rival benefiting from economies of scale.

(11 marks)

Student answer

If a larger rival has economies of scale, then it is likely that they will have lower costs of production per unit. Therefore, they would be able to charge a lower price for their product, meaning that they could undercut the small firm. There are a number of ways that a small firm could deal with this situation.

Firstly, it could accept a lower profit margin. If the economies of scale are not that big, then the small firm might be able to match the big firm on price, and still be able to make some profit. A small firm might be run by its owners, who may only be looking to make enough profit to earn a living – they might not mind too much about the lower profits, as long as they have enough.

Secondly, if the firm has to charge a higher price, it will have to justify this by adding more value. It could do this by looking to serve a niche in the market, perhaps by concentrating on higher quality and not worrying too much about price. Bang and Olafson probably don't get economies of scale, but they are still profitable, because they have a niche in the market.

Overall then, it depends on how big the economies of scale are. If they are big, the firm may have to go for a niche to compete. If not, they could compete normally, and just make less profit. This might be a problem eventually.

Marker's comments

This candidate has been well taught – the answer has a clear structure, which really adds to the overall quality. There is an introduction which looks at key issues in the question, separate numbered points, and then an attempt at an evaluative conclusion.

The answer opens well, with the candidate being careful to explain what he or she means and developing the points ('because …'; 'therefore …'). In the two main paragraphs, the points are well argued, even if the language is a little simplistic in places. Particularly impressive is the candidate's use of material from other sections of the specification ('value added') to support their answer.

The conclusion sums up the argument well, although it probably doesn't add that much to the mark – there is a good point right at the end, which unfortunately there wasn't time to develop.

Nevertheless, this is a high quality answer containing evidence of evaluation ('it depends how big economies of scale are'; 'if it is a small firm, …').

Mark: Content 2/2, Application & Analysis 6/6, Evaluation 2/3. Total = 10

Analyse the ways in which a firm might increase its capacity utilisation.

(9 marks)

Student answer

There are many ways in which capacity utilisation could be increased. The firm could buy new machines which would mean that it could make more, increasing its capacity utilisation. However, it might have to get more buildings to put the machines in, which might cause diseconomies of scale due to communication problems. Also, workers in a bigger firm might not be so motivated, and it might be hard to co-ordinate all the different machines, increasing costs instead of reducing them.

Alternatively, the firm could get more people, which would allow it to make more. This might cause problems if new workers don't get on with the existing workers, causing a culture clash.

Overall, the firm could either increase machines or labour to increase its capacity utilisation, but it would depend on the size of the firm, the state of the economy and what market it is in as to which would be best.

Marker's comments

There are several problems with this answer, but the most basic is that it confuses **capacity** with **capacity utilisation**. Buying more machinery should increase a firm's capacity to produce, but unless the demand is there, capacity utilisation might actually fall.

Other problems are the lack of analysis – points aren't really explained or related back to the question – and the learned 'it depends' conclusion, which is worth no marks because there is no explanation attached. And it isn't really required for an analysis question in any case.

Mark: Content 0/2, Application 0/3, Analysis 0/4. Total = 0

Discuss how important the generation of economies of scale might be to a firm's long-term success.

(11 marks)

Student answer

Economies of scale can be really important for a firm, because they can help to reduce unit costs. For example, a larger firm will be able to buy in bulk, which might help the firm to get a discount from its suppliers. Provided the cost of storing all of the extra material is not too great, this should help to keep down the firm's costs.

A reduction in costs is very important in many markets, because it can be passed on to the customer as lower prices – this may give the firm a competitive advantage. Customers will hopefully see the firm as providing better value for money, unless they think the price cut means lower quality.

If the firm does not pass on the cost saving to the customer then it will make more profit. This can be reinvested into more research and development or more up-to-date equipment, which might give the firm an advantage in the long term. Which the firm does might depend on whether the firm has a long or short-term focus.

Overall, economies of scale are very important to a firm, because they can give it a price edge, or enable it to invest more in its future.

Marker's comments

This is a reasonable answer. In its favour, is that for the most part it relates to the question – one problem is that the candidate drifts into a learned short term/long term evaluation that is not related back to the question. The main weakness, is that although the answer explains why economies of scale are important, it doesn't say how important, and it doesn't look at what is meant by success. Consequently, although there is some evidence of evaluation at the end of the first paragraph, the mark would be limited. Analysis though is quite solid – points are explained, and generally developed.

Mark: Content 2/2, Application & Analysis 4/6, Evaluation 1/3. Total = 7

Consider the likely problems a firm might face when trying to increase its capacity utilisation.

(11 marks)

Student answer

A firm wanting to increase capacity utilisation can do so in several ways.

Firstly, it can reduce its capacity by rationalising. This means getting rid of unnecessary capacity, like unused machines, so that the firm doesn't have to pay to service them. This might be a problem though if it sold too many – if demand went up, the firm might not be able to meet it. This might mean losing customers or investing in new equipment, which would be a waste if it had just got rid of some.

Secondly, it could try to increase sales, say by advertising. The problem is that this costs money and, in any case, the effects might not last very long. If utilisation has been low for a long time – it's not just a blip – the firm might need to do something a bit more serious, like redesign its product.

Alternatively, it could look for subcontracting work, like making own brand products for supermarkets. This would use capacity, but could be a problem, because it might damage its own sales.

Marker's comments

This is a difficult answer to mark because it doesn't really answer the question directly. The candidate focuses more on how to increase utilisation than on the problems faced. Nevertheless, each of the methods identified does come with a limitation, and those limitations deal with some of the problems.

There would certainly be no marks for evaluation – there is very little judgement shown, but the answer is fairly analytical in places, and does answer the question indirectly.

Mark: Content 2/2, Application & Analysis 3/6, Evaluation 0/3. Total = 5

End of section questions

1 Analyse the likely problems facing a firm wanting to increase the scale of its operations.

(9 marks)

2 Discuss the circumstances under which mergers are likely to generate more economies than diseconomies of scale.

(11 marks)

3 Does the presence of economies of scale mean that governments should relax restrictions on monopolies and mergers?

(11 marks)

4 To what extent is an increase in the size of a firm likely to benefit consumers?

(11 marks)

5 Examine the benefits a firm might generate as a result of an increase in the scale of its operations.

(9 marks)

6 Discuss the factors which might determine the optimum scale of operations for a firm.

(11 marks)

7 Analyse the likely problems facing a firm with high levels of capacity utilisation.

(9 marks)

8 Analyse the likely implications for a firm which has low levels of capacity utilisation.

(9 marks)

9 Examine the factors that might determine a firm's level of capacity.

(11 marks)

10 Discuss the likely impact on a firm of an increase in the scale of its operations.

(11 marks)

Essays

1 'Given the significance of economies of scale, there is no place for small firms in the twenty-first century.' Evaluate this statement.

(40 marks)

2 Rimet Ltd produces footballs and has operated at 100% capacity utilisation for 2 years. The managing director is considering purchasing additional manufacturing capacity at an industrial estate two miles from the main factory. Discuss the factors that might be taken into account when making this decision.

(40 marks)

3 'In business, small is beautiful.' Discuss.

(40 marks)

4 Consider the circumstances under which a growing firm might be able to avoid diseconomies of scale.

(40 marks)

5 Igo ltd has operated at an average of 55% capacity utilisation for 5 years. Discuss the factors that might determine how Igo should respond to this situation.

(40 marks)

Summary chart

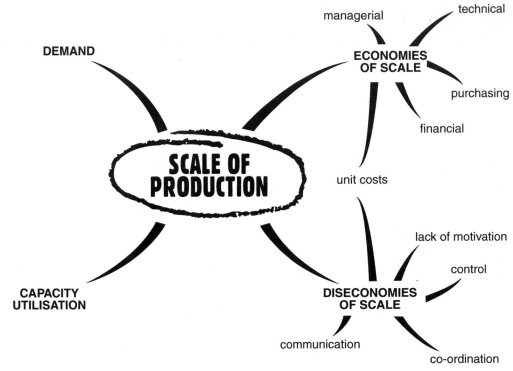

Figure 3.3 Scale of production

Quality

What is good quality?

A quality good or service is one which meets customers requirements and is '**fit for purpose**'. This means that the product does what customers expect it to do for the price, i.e. it represents good, or even excellent, value for money. Although we tend to associate quality with high priced items the fact that an item is expensive does not in itself guarantee that it is good quality – if you pay several hundred pounds for a new washing machine and find it breaks down within a few weeks you would not regard this as acceptable. A high price is, therefore, no assurance in itself of good quality. At the same time, it is perfectly possible for a cheap product to be excellent quality: a newspaper may cost less than a pound but if it has everything in it that you want, you may well regard this as good value for money; similarly you may only pay a few pence for a pencil but if it does all you expect it to you might be very pleased with your purchase. The quality of an item, therefore, refers to the benefits it provides in relation to the benefits customers expect it to provide for the price.

> **A good quality item does not have to be expensive – it has to be 'fit for purpose'.**

PROGRESS CHECK

Consider the view that the more expensive a product is, the better quality it is.

What is a quality organisation?

KEY POINTS

A quality organisation is more likely to:

- be open to change
- seek to learn from others
- invest in training
- be market orientated
- have visonary leaders
- be dynamic and innovative.

George Binney, a quality consultant, identifies four key characteristics of the companies which have been successful in becoming **quality organisations**. Managers must be capable of:

1 Forthright and listening leadership – leaders must be assertive about standards and objectives, making clear that quality is non-negotiable and that the customer is the number one priority. At the same time, leaders need to listen to and act on employees' views, and draw on the knowledge and skills of people at all levels.

2 Provoking not imposing change – this means that people throughout the organ-

isation need to be involved in change so they have a strong sense of ownership of new ways of working.

3 Integrating quality into the very fabric of business – quality must be seen as the responsibility of everyone, not some specialist department or team. Employee appraisals should emphasise customer satisfaction and the selection of staff must focus on their attitudes to quality.

4 Learning by doing – time and space has to be allowed for learning and experimentation. People have to be allowed to try ideas out without fear of retribution if they make errors.

A quality organisation is **dynamic**; it is continually seeking to improve. It is also likely to consist of passionate believers in the quality message: people who believe in the importance of the customer and the need to focus everything on customer requirements.

Quality-oriented firms are also likely to be **learning organisations**; they will recognise the importance of improving what they do and of learning how to do things better. They are likely to have an open culture in which contact with other firms is encouraged and in which managers are expected to innovate and try out new things. Quality organisations also place employees at the very heart of what they do – after all, long-term, sustainable improvement must come from the employees themselves. At the same time, the vision, the commitment and the allocation of resources must come from the management.

FACT FILE

'There is so much talk about involvement of employees, quality of work life, communications, and other poetic words. What is needed is involvement of management; get the management involved. Employees will become involved, the quality of life will improve, once management takes on the job of restoring dignity to the hourly worker.'
Source: W. Edwards Deming
Quality, Productivity and Competitive Position

PROGRESS CHECK

How do you think you could recognise whether an organisation was committed to improving its quality?

KEY POINTS

A firm is more likely to offer good quality if:

- it is market rather than product oriented
- it has a good understanding of customer needs
- it believes in the importance of customers
- it strives to meet customer needs on an ongoing basis
- it is in a highly competitive environment and has to differentiate itself.

The traditional approach and the modern approach to quality

The traditional approach

Once the product and the production process have been designed, the firm has to ensure that it produces its goods and services in a consistent manner and that, when they reach the customer, there are no defects. The traditional approach to achieving quality focuses on inspecting the finished products. This is known as a **quality control system**. This approach assumes that production will inevitably involve some defects; the role of the quality control function is to identify the products which do have faults and to prevent them getting to the customer. Quality control is, therefore, placed at the end of the process and acts as a filter mechanism to ensure the customer does not receive faulty products.

Traditional approach — Production process ⟶ | Quality control | ⟶ 👤 Customer

Quality control occurs at the end of the production process

Modern approach — Production process ⟶ 👤→👤→👤→👤→👤→👤   External customer

Internal customers

Quality control is built into each stage

Figure 4.1 Traditional and modern approaches to quality

The modern approach

Using the modern approach to quality managers attempt to prevent mistakes occurring in the first place, rather than finding them once they have occurred. Resources are put into ensuring that the product is perfect at each stage of the process, so that by the time it leaves the production line it does not actually need checking.

> **Quality occurs when people get it right first time; not when they put it right later on.**

A firm can prevent defects occurring by:

■ designing a product which is relatively simple to make

■ designing a process which is relatively simple to use and monitor

■ involving employees in the process and using their ideas for improvement

■ empowering employees to reject any work which is passed to them that has defects; this places a responsibility on every person or team in the organisation to get it right first time

■ empowering employees to check their own work and rectify any errors, i.e. making employees accountable for their own quality.

Internal and external customers

The modern approach to quality requires all employees to be responsible for the quality of their own work and to meet the needs of their customers. A customer is anyone for whom you do work; this means there are internal customers – customers within the organisation – as well as the external customers who are the people that actually buy the product or service. All employees have to consider the people who are next in the **quality chain** (i.e. the people they pass their work to), identify their requirements and attempt to meet these every time.

FACT FILE

The traditional approach to quality attempts to cure the problem once it has occurred. The modern approach tries to prevent mistakes occurring in the first place. The 'prevention' or 'cure' debate occurs in many areas of life. Should the police put resources into trying to prevent crimes occurring (e.g. putting more police on the streets) or on solving crimes once they have occurred (e.g putting more resources into rapid response teams)? Should the National Health Service focus on preventing diseases and illness occurring (through e.g. anti-smoking education and vaccinations) or on curing people once they are ill (e.g. by investing more in hospitals)?

> **Quality involves meeting the needs of all your customers, not just the one who buy the final products. Customers are internal as well as external.**

Is prevention better than inspection?

KEY POINTS

Firms using the modern approach to quality are more likely to:

- invest in prevention techniques
- empower employees to inspect their own work
- design processes which build in quality
- consider the requirements of both internal and external customers.

Can zero defects ever be achieved?

A key element of the modern approach to quality is the target of 'zero defects'. Organisations must constantly seek to produce a good or service which is absolutely perfect. Many people are very dismissive of this target, arguing that it is impossible to achieve and so there is no point setting it. Believers in the modern approach to quality management would argue that the zero defects target is a valuable one because it reflects a way of thinking and sets a challenging, inspiring, overall goal for everyone in the organisation. Even today, relatively poor performance occurs in many organisations in the UK; consciously or subconsciously managers set 'acceptable levels of quality' – once these have been achieved employees do not try any harder to improve. For example, managers might decide that it is acceptable for 5% of the goods produced to have mistakes; they only get worried if the level of rejects rises above this 5% level. This approach to quality demonstrates an underlying belief that mistakes are inevitable. By comparison, the new approach to quality starts from the belief that mistakes cannot be allowed to happen and that everyone must work towards preventing them. Think of the airbags in a car: we do not work on the assumption that they will work most of the time but not all of the time. When we travel by plane we do want to get on an aircraft which will fly safely most of the time but sometimes have problems. In both these cases products are built to work every time without failure.

To achieve quality of a similar standard in all our products, we must design them assuming that no defects are allowed. Of course, in reality mistakes will sometimes occur. The key thing is not to *accept* these and dismiss them as 'inevitable' or 'tolerable', but to look closely at why they occurred and attempt to prevent them occurring again. Every customer complaint, every reject item and every instance of a good being returned should be examined carefully to identify why it happened and how it could be prevented next time.

The philosophy of modern quality management is that 'quality is a journey'; firms may never quite achieve zero defects but they must continually seek to improve what they do to move ever closer.

FACT FILE

Shigeo Shingo is a famous quality guru. Shingo's motto was 'Those who are not dissatisfied will never make any progress'. Shingo developed the Poya-Yoke or 'Defects=0' concept. The basic idea is that the production process should be stopped whenever a defect occurs; employees must identify the cause and prevent the same defect happening again.

Do you think it is realistic or useful to set a target of zero defects?

Is quality expensive?

The traditional view

If you take the traditional view of quality and put resources into quality control, you would almost certainly regard quality as an unfortunate necessity. You would prefer not to have a quality control department, but recognise that you need one! You would also regard quality control as an unfortunate expense: to find the mistakes which you think occur inevitably in any process, you must invest in inspection mechanisms. The more mistakes you want to find, the more you must invest. Under this system better quality means more inspection, which means more cost. Quality is, therefore, seen as expensive.

The modern view

Using the modern approach, quality is achieved through prevention. This costs money initially, because people need to be trained, working practices have to be changed and new equipment may be required. In the long term, however, there are less faults, less wastage and less scrap. This means that long-term costs may fall.

PROGRESS CHECK

Explain how investing to improve quality can actually save money in the long run.

The benefits of improving quality

An improvement in quality will reduce costs. It also provides customers with more of the benefits that they want with less faults, and this should lead to higher sales. With more sales and lower unit costs the overall return on capital employed should increase.

Costs may fall for a number of reasons including:

- less wastage (e.g. fewer scrap products)
- less downtime (i.e. less time spent waiting for machinery to be fixed)
- reduced legal costs because the business is less likely to be sued by customers who received faulty products
- fewer returned goods (the firm avoids all the costs associated with this)
- less dissatisfied customers.

The benefits of improved quality clearly include:

- more satisfied customers
- high levels of customer goodwill

- an ability to differentiate the firm's offerings from those of other firms producing lower quality goods

- higher sales.

Japanese influence on quality

Much of the underlying philosophy of the modern approach to quality and the techniques involved originate in Japan. In the late 1960s, most Western firms were concentrating on producing as much as possible to benefit from economies of scale; they accepted that this would lead to more faults and believed that the only solution was to spend more on inspection. In the 1980s, Japanese firms were able to produce goods which were not only cheaper, but offered more benefits than their Western competitors. As a result, Japanese firms gained control of a wide range of markets, particularly consumer electronics products such as televisions, hi-fis and video recorders.

> **PROGRESS CHECK**
>
> In what ways might a firm benefit from improving its quality?

Achieving quality

To improve the quality of its product or service an organisation must identify its customer requirements. This means that quality is closely linked to the idea of market orientation. To provide something that people regard as quality, you need to understand their needs and wants; this requires marketing research.

The firm must design a production system which can deliver the desired benefits at an appropriate price and still be profitable. This means that managers must consider issues such as the design of the product and process to ensure that the investment is financially viable. The design stage is absolutely critical to the success of any new product. By carefully planning the specifications of the product and the way in which it is to be made, a firm can prevent many of the problems which often occur later if no one has prepared for them.

To achieve quality requires:

- commitment from managers

- training for employees

- the involvement of employees in decision-making.

- investment in technology and equipment.

> **PROGRESS CHECK**
>
> Discuss the ways in which a firm might improve its quality.

FACT FILE

In the 1970s some Japanese companies thought that Western companies would never manage to change to improve their quality. A statement by Konosuke Matsushito attracted considerable publicity: 'We are going to win and the industrial West is going to lose – there is nothing much you can do about it, because the reasons for your failure are within yourselves. For you, the essence of management is getting the ideas out of the heads of bosses into the hands of labour. For us the core of management is precisely the art of mobilising and pulling together the intellectual resources of all employees in the service of the firm. Only by drawing on the combined brain power of all its employees can a firm face up to the turbulence and constraints of today's environment.'

FACT FILE

In 1995 the UK factory of Timken, the US's biggest maker of rolling bearings for industry, first began to brainstorm. Shop-floor workers were encouraged to come up with new suggestions. The result was 1000 ideas for improving production! The ideas from the brainstorming were combined with experience gained from the group's other worldwide manufacturing sites. Changes in ways of working have led to productivity gains at its plant near Northampton of around 10% a year.

Quality techniques

The quality cycle

Achieving quality cannot be hit or miss; firms need to define precisely which targets to hit, develop processes to achieve them and then measure the results. If you visit 'quality' organisations you will usually see charts, tables and graphs throughout the factory, as teams measure their performance against agreed targets. If the targets are not achieved, the process must be altered until they are.

Once a firm has consistently met a given set of targets, it must set even higher targets for itself and then set about achieving these. Quality is, therefore, an ongoing process.

This approach to quality can be seen in the PDCA cycle developed by W. Edwards Deming. To achieve better quality, managers and teams must:

■ **Plan** what they want to achieve

■ **Develop** the means of achieving this

■ **Check** whether it has been achievd

■ **Act** if it has not.

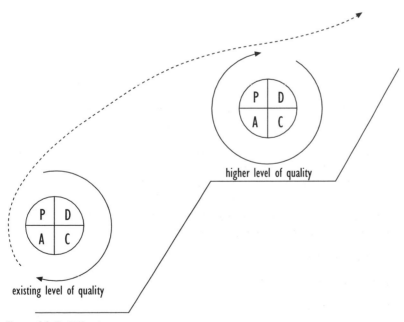

Figure 4.2 The PDCA cycle

Managers develop a means of improving quality. Once this is achieved, new, higher targets are then set.

Benchmarking

Benchmarking is a process by which firms assess their own ways of doing things against the best in the world. Organisations choose a particular aspect of their business activity and compare the way they do it and the results they have achieved with the firms which lead the world in this particular area. Benchmarking is usually undertaken when an organisation realises it is underperforming in a specific activity. For example, it might try to find out how other firms develop their products so quickly, how they deliver their goods so reliably or how they respond so quickly to customer enquiries.

An organisation which undertakes benchmarking must be willing to learn from the best in the world. The best may or may not be in the same industry. For example, firms which want to improve customer service could learn a great deal from the Disney Corporation, whether or not they are in the entertainment or leisure business.

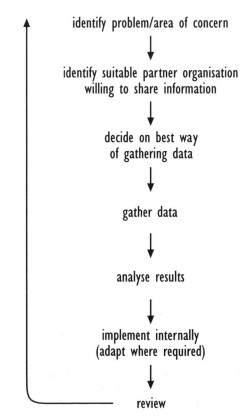

Figure 4.3 The benchmarking process

The difficulties of benchmarking

However, benchmarking does bring with it many problems. Not least is the difficulty of getting people within the firm to realise the need to improve and making them look outside of the organisation for solutions to their problems. In many organisations there is an air of complacency – managers are often reluctant to accept that things could be better because this implies that they are not doing it correctly at the moment; naturally, some people regard benchmarking as a criticism of their performance. In fact poor performance is often to do with the way things are being done, rather than any lack of individual effort. Even if people do accept the need to change, they tend to think they can solve it themselves and are wary of looking outside of the firm for solutions.

Another problem with benchmarking is finding a world-class firm willing to share information on how it undertakes a particular process. Other organisations may not want outsiders to know how they do things; after all, if they are the best in the world, they may want to keep this position and could be reluctant to show others how to do it as well ! One way of overcoming this problem is to benchmark against firms in different industries, so that companies do not pose a direct threat to one another. Some companies form an association of firms who all share data in different aspects of their businesses, so everyone is learning from everyone else. However, finding suitable and willing partners can be difficult.

Having found a benchmarking partner, the next stage is to gather the data and analyse it. This can also cause problems – what is the best way to collect information? How long should the firm spend on this? What do the findings actually mean?

KEY POINTS

A firm is more likely to achieve high quality if:

- it has a well trained and motivated workforce
- it has a clear definition of customer needs
- it spends a relatively long time on the design stage.

Once the data has been gathered and analysed, a firm has to try and implement the methods of the world-class firm. It is important to remember that it is not possible simply to take one set of techniques from a firm and impose them on another organisation; the history, the culture, the employment relations record and the resources of the second company may be very different from the first. The methods and techniques have to be adjusted accordingly.

The support of the workforce is also crucial – they must be involved in the changes because they are the ones who will implement them.

Benchmarking can be tremendously useful; after all, it is easier to learn from someone who has already been through the problems of developing and introducing a process, rather than having to do it yourself for the first time with no outside experience. Through benchmarking, firms can benefit from a tried and tested set of procedures. This is not a case of trying out something new without any idea of whether it will work – managers know it has been extremely successful already.

The value of benchmarking depends on:

- whether the firm has selected the right process to benchmark (if a firm has decided to improve its handling of customer eqnuiries when in fact the real problem is its distribution service, benchmarking may be of limited use)

- whether the firm can find a suitable organisation to benchmark against

- whether the data is collected and analysed effectively

- whether the methods are implemented successfully

- whether employees are involved in the process of change and have the required skills.

To be successful, benchmarking must be introduced carefully and new processes must be well thought out. The management must provide sufficient resources and support, and the new techniques must be introduced within the context and framework of the firm's existing operations.

How do firms decide what to benchmark?

Total Quality Management (TQM)

Total Quality Management is an approach which seeks to involve every employee in the process of improving quality. It stresses that everyone in the organisation contributes to its success:

- Designers must design a product and process which are efficient and which build-in quality.

- The marketing function must identify customer needs.

- The production function must produce products which meet the set specifications.

- The finance function must ensure the firm has the funds it needs as and when it needs them.

- Human Resources must ensure the firm has the right people at the right time.

- The Information Technology services department must provide information when it is required.

- The sales department must deal with customers orders and requests efficiently.

All employees produce work for customers (whether internal and external). They must identify their customer requirements and develop processes to achieve a zero defect performance. TQM is as much a philosophy as a set of techniques; it requires everyone to think of everything in terms of customer needs. Everyone, all the time, must examine their actions, decide on the extent to which these meet customer requirements and develop methods of improving their quality over time.

This approach to business is, in some ways, exhausting! It means workers must measure continuously what they are achieving and always seek to improve their performance. It is easy to become satisfied with what has been achieved so far and not push to set ever higher targets; TQM does not allow this. Whatever you are doing now, it could be done better!

In what way is Total Quality Management a philosophy?

BS 5750

BS 5750 is a UK quality award given to firms which have a proven system of quality; the European equivalent is ISO 9000. To achieve this award, firms must set quality targets, develop a system for achieving these and take action if they are not achieved. In other words, firms must have an ongoing system in which they are measuring continuously their performance relative to set targets. This sort of firm is clearly concerned about its standards and recognises the importance of measuring its existing performance. It is likely to be customer oriented and provide a high quality service. As a result, some businesses actively look for suppliers which have BS 5750 awards because this indicates that they believe in providing a quality product or service. Having the BS 5750 award can, therefore, be used in a firm's marketing and can help it to win new orders.

However, the BS 5750 award does not in itself *guarantee* that a firm actually produces a high quality service or product. The award shows that a firm consistently meets its own targets – it does not guarantee that these targets are worth hitting! A firm could set relatively easy targets to hit in terms of customer service, delivery and reliability and still gain the award.

The value of BS 5750 depends on whether a firm's customers value it or not. Its value also depends on how many other firms have also gained the award. In one sense, it may be more desirable to be one of a few firms to have this award as it helps to differentiate the business; on the other hand, the more firms that have gained BS 5750, the more it helps to raise awareness of the award.

The value of the award also depends on what it costs to achieve in terms of bureaucracy and paperwork. To gain BS 5750 a firm must be able to show that it is regularly measuring its performance relative to the set targets; this involves high levels of record keeping which some organisations have found very time consuming.

To the customer, the value of the award depends on the underlying targets that the firm has set itself rather the award itself, although the award is likely to reflect a particular way of thinking within the organisation. If the firm has bothered to introduce the systems to gain the award, it will probably set quite demanding targets.

KEY TERM

BS 5750
is 'a way of describing the capability of a system to produce goods or services to a specification'.

FACT FILE

Over 54,000 UK firms can boast an award in the ISO 9000 series.

FACT FILE

The importance of quality is now recognised in a number of prestigious quality awards in different countries such as:

- The Deming Prize (Japan)
- The Malcolm Baldridge National Quality Awards (USA)
- The European Quality Award (Europe).

PROGRESS CHECK

What determines the value of BS 5750 to a firm?

KEY POINTS

BS 5750 is more likely to be useful to a firm if:

- customers value the award
- it differentiates the firm from the competition
- the system leads to cost savings
- the system helps build employee commitment to quality
- the targets are meaningful.

Kaizen

Kaizen is a Japanese word which means 'continuous improvement'. The kaizen approach is to increase a firm's competitiveness on an ongoing basis through a series of small improvements. Rather than looking all the time for major investments, the advocates of kaizen highlight that dramatic improvements can occur through a series of relatively small steps. If a firm manages to improve just one aspect of the work process each week, over time this can have significant effect the overall performance. Kaizen can help the firm to become more efficient and to provide a better quality service.

To be successful, kaizen relies on the commitment of the whole workforce. Improvements come from those who do the work. The kaizen system can only be introduced in an environment which encourages suggestions from employees, and which sets aside time and resources for them to participate and to present their ideas. It is unlikely to be effective in a top down system where the workforce is used to being told what to do and where management is authoritarian rather than democratic.

Firms seeking to benefit from an approach of continuous improvement will usually establish 'kaizen groups'; these are teams of employees which develop new ideas and systems to reduce costs and add value. These groups are self financing over time, although they have to be funded at first.

Although kaizen offers many potential benefits (if implemented correctly), all it actually does is improve an *existing* system. On some occasions more radical thinking may be required. If the system itself is out of date or has been surpassed by new technology, kaizen is unlikely to uncover this. Similarly, if a major shift in the firm's strategy is required, the kaizen approach will not bring this about; this will require senior management to identify the changes in market conditions and to identify how the firm should respond.

In recent years, several commentators have argued that firms need to examine their activities from first principles; instead of trying to improve what they have, they should question their whole approach to the business they are in. They should forget the way they do things at the moment and ask themselves how they would do it if they started from scratch. This process is known as **re-engineering** and can result in a major restructuring of a firm's activities.

> **Kaizen takes what you have and tries to make it better. Re-engineering takes what you have, throws it away and starts again!**

What factors might determine the success of the kaizen process?

Philip Crosby's ideas

One of the leading quality gurus of recent years is Philip Crosby. His work includes the book s *Quality is Free* in 1979 and *Quality without Tears* in 1984. Crosby introduced the Four Absolutes of Quality which summarise many of the key elements of the modern approach to quality.

FACT FILE

Cummins Engine of the US runs a plant in Daventry making diesel engines for power generation. The plant has a team of people who visit its suppliers to school them in new thinking, such as kaizen.

KEY POINTS

Kaizen is more likely to work:

- if employees are encouraged to participate
- in an open, innovative culture
- when the management style is democratic
- when employer—employee relations are positive
- over the long term

KEY POINTS

Kaizen is more likely to be important:

- over time rather than in the short run
- if employees are committed to quality
- if management invest resources and time into improvement
- if other firms are not improving.

His Four Absolutes are:

1 Quality is defined as conformance to requirements, not as 'goodness' or 'elegance' (i.e. quality involves meeting customer requirements).
2 The system for causing quality is prevention, not appraisal (i.e. the aim is to get things right first time, not fix it later).
3 The performance standard must be Zero Defects, not 'that's close enough'.
4 The measurement of quality is the Price of Non-Conformance (i.e. you should think about how much you save by preventing poor quality rather than simply looking at what you spend to achieve high quality).

A particularly important part of Crosby's message is that investing in quality *saves* money rather than *costs* money. He claims that most companies that spend around 20% of their revenue doing things wrong, and then having to do them over again. Investing in preventing mistakes saves these costs, i.e. it can actually save money.

FACT FILE

In 1999, the Freudenberg and NOK Group's LaGrange facility was chosen as a finalist in America's Best Plants competition because of its performance in several areas including:

- customer reject rates of three parts per million
- warranty costs at 0% of sales
- customer retention at 100% over the past 5 years
- On-time delivery rates of 99.3%
- A 69% reduction in order-to-ship time over the past 5 years
- A 47% decrease in scrap percentage of sales since 1995
- A 31% improvement in total inventory turns since 1995.

By conducting 260 kaizens between 1995 and 1998, the facility has been a major contributor to the company's recognition in 1999 as the the first automotive supplier to surpass 12,000 kaizen projects.

PROGRESS CHECK

In what ways can improving quality save money?

How important is quality?

Ultimately, the ability to provide a quality service must be a key objective for all organisations. If a firm is to survive in the long term it must offer its customers excellent value for money. However, the relative importance of quality will vary from organisation to organisation and depending on the circumstances. If, for example, a firm operates in a protected market with relatively limited competition, there will be less pressure to meet customer requirements.

This protection could come in the form of:

■ legal protection (for example, the government may have established a state-owned monopoly)

■ cost barriers which prevent competitors entering the market

■ control over suppliers or distributors

■ a technological advantage which creates a unique selling point (USP) meaning that competitors cannot follow easily in the short run. Some software companies are said to have knowingly launched products even though they have not been absolutely error free. Provided they feel there will not be too many complaints, they think it is better to get the products out on the market first, maintaining their position and staying ahead of the competition, and fixing the problems later.

The importance of quality will also depend on whether the firm is aiming for short-term or long-term success, and on whether it relies on customers returning to buy

FACT FILE

Duracell has developed its own continuous improvement programme through teamwork called X'Cell. X'Cell aims to improve both product and process quality. A organisation-sponsored, cross-functional and cross-hierarchical team, consisting of six to eight members, runs the X'Cell programme. The team's task is to solve problems and find solutions through a structured problem-solving methodology.

things again in the future. In the short term, a firm may be able to get away with poor quality; if, however, it aims to rely on long-term, repeat business from customers, it must ensure they are satisfied and feel they are getting value for money.

In recent years, the degree of competiton in most markets has increased. In some cases this has been due to **privatisation** and **deregulation**; in other cases, it is due to the removal of trade barriers, open up new export markets and creating potential new competitors. Many commentators now talk of global markets in which firms are competing worldwide. This means UK firms are now competing head to head with the best in the world to a greater extent than in the past – this makes it even more important to provide excellent quality.

Quality is becoming increasingly significant because customers are becoming more demanding, and are better informed about their rights and the various choices open to them. Developments such as the Internet, for example, make it much easier for customers to compare prices and the benefits offered by different firms. This places greater pressure on firms to provide better quality products and services.

However, whilst quality in general is becoming more significant, this does not mean every firm has a systematic approach to improving quality, or that they necessarily adopt formal practices such as kaizen groups. In some firms, it may just be part of the firm's culture, rather than part of the formal planning processs.

Is quality equally important to all firms?

Is the quality revolution just a fad?

The last 20 years have seen an incredible shift in many producers' views of quality. In the past, it was generally seen as the job of a relatively small quality control department to check things. Quality control was an unfortunate expense and, ultimately, was not given much importance within the firm. For many organisations, especially ones such as Rank Xerox, Toyota and Unipart, the push for quality now dominates their activities and thinking. It is seen as a means of reducing costs, and differentiating their goods and services from the competition. It can help win business and keep customers. Not all firms in the West have adopted techniques such as kaizen or TQM, but there has certainly been a move towards thinking much more about the quality of the goods and services provided in relation to customer needs. There has also been greater awareness of the role that employees and suppliers can play in improving quality. The change in approach has been so significant and so noticeable that many have labelled it a 'quality revolution'. Critics, however, point to the large number of firms which still do not think along these lines and suggest that, even for the ones that do, it is merely a fad. In some cases this may be true – managers are looking constantly for ways to revitalise their organisations and ideas such as TQM can do just this. Whether or not techniques like TQM end up as a fad is really down to the managers – do they keep providing the resources and support needed to improve? Do they lead by example? Do they keep monitoring the results so that there is a sense of an ongoing journey, rather than a one-off campaign?

In a number of cases, short-term demand may lead managers to neglect their quality initiatives – for example, in a slump the priority may be seen as increasing immediate sales, rather than building long-term quality. Also, sheer familiarity can breed boredom – the push for zero defects may be exciting at first, but three of four years later employees and managers may be looking for another programme to focus on. However, there is no reason at all why the interest in quality should be a fad, provided managers lead the way. It is perhaps inevitable, however, that the media and business writers will move on to something else, because they are constantly looking for new approaches and new ideas to interest their readers and viewers.

KEY POINTS

Quality is more likely to be important when:

- competition is high
- customers are very demanding
- competitors are improving their quality
- the firm is aiming for long-term success.

PROGRESS CHECK

What determines whether the quality revolution is a fad or not?

KEY POINTS

The quality revolution is less likely to be a fad if:

- it has been shown to be successful in the past
- managers are committed to it
- firms take a long-term view of success.

Summary chart

Figure 4.4 Quality

Approaching exam questions: quality

Assess the possible benefits of suddenly introducing kaizen groups into an organisation.

(40 marks)

This is an 'assess' question and so needs arguments for and against, then a conclusion. Specific reference should be made to the fact that kaizen groups are being introduced and students should take account of the word 'suddenly'.

The potential benefits of kaizen groups are:

■ generation of cost-saving ideas

■ revenue-producing ideas

■ they can contribute to better employment relations

■ they can contribute to a culture of improvement

■ they can lead to a competitive advantage.

However, when introducing such groups candidates would want to consider factors such as:

■ the way in which they are explained to employees

■ the employees' perception of them

■ the resources allocated to them

■ whether results are expected in the short term or whether management is willing to wait for the benefits to show.

The fact that the introduction of these groups is *sudden* may mean that the project is less likely to be successful – one might expect new techniques to be introduced gradually throughout the organisation, learning as the firm progresses. However, success again depends on how the implementation is done, and the resources and managerial commitment.

Is improving quality inevitably expensive?

(40 marks)

This is a fairly standard question. A good answer will consider the case for and against, and then question the use of the term 'inevitably'. In many ways, the question requires candidates to consider the traditional and modern approaches to quality.

According to the traditional approach quality is expensive because:

■ it involves spending on inspection

■ to improve quality requires more inspection; this costs more money.

On the other hand, better quality means:

☐ fewer mistakes

☐ less scrap

☐ less wastage

☐ higher levels of customer satisfaction (and so more revenue).

Overall, it will depend on whether the benefits of better quality exceed the costs involved (either inspection or prevention costs). It may also depend on the time period involved – improving quality may require investment to begin with, but may provide more benefits over a long time.

Improving quality is certainly likely to incur costs to start with, but may actually save money in the long run. Quality gurus such as Crosby would stress the need to consider, not just the costs of improving quality, but the costs which occur if quality is poor, i.e the costs of non-conformance (the cost of returned goods and customer dissatisfaction).

Are internal customers more important than external customers?

(40 marks)

A good answer to this question will involve a definition of the two terms and then a discussion of their relative importance. The question is typically challenging, but the answer may be that both are important: after all, to achieve good quality for your external customers you need to meet the requirements of your internal ones as well. The whole process of adding value should be seen as a 'quality chain'. From the very start of the process, work is being passed from one stage to the next, i.e. from one customer to the next. For zero defects to be achieved, each customers' needs must be fulfilled precisely. It is not a question of one group being more important – all customers matter!

Assess the potential benefits of Total Quality Management to an organisation.

(40 marks)

This question requires an outline of the benefits of Total Quality Managment.

These could include:

☐ more satisfied customers

☐ less costs, e.g. through less waste

☐ a common sense of direction within the firm

☐ continuous improvement.

However, these benefits must be 'assessed' because of the wording of the question. An answer which simply claims that TQM is beneficial would not achieve a particularly high grade. A good answer would might consider:

☐ *how* TQM has been introduced

☐ the level of support from management

■ the resources allocated to improving quality

■ the level of commitment from employeees

■ the costs involved in the TQM process

■ the level of bureaucracy.

Student answers

To what extent does good quality depend mainly on employees?

(11 marks)

Student answer

'Quality' means top of the range. If something is quality it is very good. A Rolex watch is quality. This involves employees because they make the product . To make the best, you need the best. If you have bad employees, the things you make will be bad, so employees are really important. You need good employees, otherwise there will be lots of mistakes. This means quality will be bad. If you have the best, you will have the finest products in the world and this means you will win.

Marker's comments

This is a very simplistic answer. It does not reveal any real understanding of what quality actually means – it seems to assume that 'quality' means 'expensive', which is a common mistake. It does show some understanding of how employees can contribute to better quality, but this is not explained properly. It is full of assertions without any supporting arguments. A good answer would have discussed the contribution that employees can make in relation to other factors.

Mark: Content 1/2, Application 0/4, Analysis 0/3. Total = 1

Discuss the problems a firm may face when introducing kaizen groups into the organisation.

(11 marks)

Student answer

Kaizen groups are intended to improve the way a firm works. This could involve improvements to the product and the process itself, i.e. what is being made and how it is being made. Kaizen groups involve employees making suggestions about how improvements could be made in their work area; the idea is that small improvements can add up to very significant gains over time.

However, when introducing these groups it is important to win over the employees. Employees may be suspicious of management – why is management asking for help and for employee participation? To some extent, the employee reaction will depend on the nature of existing employer–employee relations: if they had been good to begin with the kaizen groups might be more accepted, compared to a situation in which managers had not been getting on with the workforce.

There may also be problems if the management is not willing to invest the necessary resources to implement the ideas of the groups. Imagine if you were asked for ideas but then nothing happened. Investment may depend on the firm's financial position – in a period of poor trading managers may think that the firm cannot afford to introduce any of the ideas of the group which cost money and may simply look to make cost savings.

People may become impatient because they want sudden improvements – the gains of kaizen often take time to show through. This depends a bit on the culture of the organisation and expectation of those involved – for example, are they looking to be successful in the long term or simply looking for short-term success. Kaizen is more likely to bring long-term gains.

Marker's comments

This is an excellent answer. It shows a good understanding of the topic area and discusses the problems which might be involved. The technique is good – the candidate develops a point and then highlights when this might be more or less important.

Mark: Content 2/2, Application and Analysis 6/6, Evaluation 3/3. Total = 11

To what extent is gaining BS 5750 essential to organisations in the UK?

(11 marks)

Student answer

BS 5750 is a quality award which means that firms have excellent quality products. If you have BS 5750 you are producing some of the best goods in the world. People will want to buy the products because they are better than everyone else's. It is essential to get this award to be able to compete. Without it, you will not sell anything because nothing you do will be any good.

The award is good for marketing because you can tell people you have it and get more sales. If customers have to choose between a firm which has BS 5750 and firms which do not, they will choose one which has a government award because it will feel more secure.

Marker's comments

Not a very successful answer. The candidate does not know exactly what BS 5750 is and seems to believe it is a guarantee of quality products. Ideas are not developed or analysed well. The language is also simplistic and extreme; for example: 'Without it, you will not sell anything because nothing you do will be any good.' The student makes no attempt to question whether BS 5750 is essential or not.

Mark: Content 1/2, Application and Analysis 2/6, Evaluation 0/3. Total = 3

Discuss the view that improving quality is the number one challenge for all organisations in the twenty-first century.

(11 marks)

Student answer

Quality means 'fit for purpose', i.e. the good or service meets customers' needs. Quality is important because it can affect sales and costs. Better quality can reduce costs (e.g. through less wastage and fewer mistakes being made); it can also lead to more sales because the products have fewer faults and satisfy customers. Faced with the choice between good quality and bad quality, customers will choose the former. Good quality can lead to customer goodwill and brand loyalty; it may also enable the firm to increase its price and profit margin.

By understanding the customers' requirements – internal and external – firms can meet their needs more effectively and this should lead to more sales. It is important, therefore, to improve quality because this will improve the firm's performance. However, some firms already have good quality, so it is more important for some than others.

Marker's comments

This candidate understands what quality is and why it is important. He or she explains the possible benefits of good quality. However, no attempt is made to answer the actual question – there is no reference to the view that improving quality is the number one challenge; there is no discussion of conditions in the twenty-first century as opposed to, say, the twentieth and the candidate does not deal fully with the idea that quality is a priority for 'all' firms. Overall, a disappointing response because the candidate does not use his or her information to answer the question.

Mark: Content 2/2, Application and Analysis 3/6, Evaluation 0/3. Total = 5

End of section questions

1 'The target of zero defects can never be achieved so why bother trying?' Discuss this view.

(11 marks)

2 'Improving quality is inevitably expensive.' Discuss this view.

(11 marks)

3 Analyse the possible benefits to an organisation of improving the quality of its goods and services.

(9 marks)

4 Discuss the possible benefits of benchmarking.

(11 marks)

5 Analyse the possible problems of introducing a benchmarking system to an organisation.

(9 marks)

6 Consider the possible value of kaizen groups to an organisation.

(11 marks)

7 Discuss the possible reasons why employees might resist attempts to improve quality.

(11 marks)

8 Consider the possible reasons why it is becoming increasingly important for firms to improve their quality.

(11 marks)

9 Analyse the possible value to a firm of being awarded BS 5750.

(9 marks)

10 In a number of organisations techniques such as Total Quality Management and kaizen groups have proved short lived. Discuss the possible reasons for this.

(11 marks)

Essays

1 'Many companies have adopted slogans such as "Quality is Number One". In fact, the present interest in quality is simply a passing fad.' Discuss.

(40 marks)

2 To what extent should firms invest in improving the quality of their products and services?

(40 marks)

3 'Improving quality should be the priority of all organisations.' Discuss.

(40 marks)

4 Is it better to improve quality in small steps or with major improvements?

(40 marks)

5 'Most quality techniques originate in Japan and can never work as effectively in the UK, because the culture of business and the way that employees are treated are so different.' Discuss this view.

(40 marks)

Lean production

Introduction

Lean production is a system of production that uses a range of waste-saving measures. It has been described as achieving the greatest level of outputs from the smallest quantity of inputs. There are specific means of achieving this, such as **just-in-time production**, **simultaneous engineering** and **flexible specialisation**. However, lean production is more than a tool box of ready-made measures that can be applied to any business circumstance. Instead, lean production is more properly seen as a **philosophy of production**. It encourages all employees to be alert to wastage at all times. Through methods such as **suggestion schemes**, **quality circles** and so on, such observations are passed upwards from the shop floor to decision-makers, allowing relevant action to be taken. The continuous improvement of the production system allows the firm to improve its wastage levels on a gradual basis, rather than attempting to make large, sweeping changes at periodic intervals.

> **Lean production can reduce unit costs and increases a firm's competitiveness.**

KEY TERM

Lean production
a philosophy of production that aims to minimise inputs whilst attaining maximum outputs. Some of the techniques that can be used to develop lean production are: Total Quality Management, just-in-time production, zero defects, kaizen groups, cell production, time-based management and simultaneous engineering.

Introducing lean production

For the philosophy to work, it must be supported by the corporate culture and the organisational structures of the firm. There have been many instances where the idea of lean production has been adopted by a firm, but the anticipated benefits have failed to arise. In the vast majority of these cases it was because the firm had not put the necessary support structures into place first.

> **PROGRESS CHECK**
>
> Can lean production be applied as a cure for all the ills of a particular business?

FACT FILE

Examples of wasted time (in the sense of not adding value) include time spent walking, bending and stooping down, searching for parts or tools, moving parts and materials, reworking, inspecting, repairing, adjusting, holding ...

Support structures

The key supports required for a system of lean production to be effective are discussed below.

Communication systems

Systems are required which are flexible enough to permit the effective two-way transfer of ideas and information. The impetus for the continuous improvements implied by a lean production system must come from the factory floor. It is here that small, practical problems will be encountered and solutions can be found. Any blockage in the channels of communication would only serve to inhibit the process of improvement.

Flexibility

Every aspect of the business ought to be ready and willing to change as circumstances change around them. This applies equally to the workforce, who need to become multi-skilled so that they can take on different roles as required, to managers, who must be prepared to change any aspect of the business that is no longer aiding the business in achieving its goals, and to machinery, which must be adaptable to different products as the demand from consumers shifts.

Motivation

As well as ensuring that workers have adequate means of communications, there must be systems in place that encourage them to look for and implement potential improvements. Whether these rewards are extrinsic, in that they give a financial benefit, or intrinsic in terms of self-satisfaction or recognition, employees must be aware of the advantage of suggesting improvements.

Empowerment

Employees must be allowed to take a degree of control over their own working lives if they are to participate in a lean production system. They need to feel as though their contributions are valued, taken seriously and acted upon by their superiors if they are to be willing to put their ideas forward.

Leadership style

In the same vein, it is unlikely to be feasible to adopt an authoritarian approach to the management of a lean production system. Managers must see other employees as having a valid and valued contribution to make to the business. It is likely that lean production systems would prosper under a democratic management style.

FACT FILE

Taiichi Ohno, a leading exponent of lean production (especially JIT), identified seven types of waste:
- overproduction
- waiting
- transportation
- processing
- excessive stocks
- unnecessary motion, e.g. having to move to find parts or tools
- making defective products.

KEY POINTS

Lean production is most likely to be successful where:

- the management style is democratic
- employees are empowered
- employees are motivated
- communication is effective and two-way.

PROGRESS· CHECK

Outline the key factors that might need to be in place for lean production to be successfully implemented.

Does lean production work?

The ideas behind a lean production system have been gaining much ground amongst business academics for many years. The theory is one that makes intuitive sense: reducing waste *must* lead to financial benefits, and accepting the contributions of workers fits in with the more widely-known motivation theories. Critics of the theory, however, point out that firms in the UK have been slow to take the system on board and, of those that have, success has not always been assured.

As with many business theories, it does not provide a single answer for every different problem faced by every different firm. There is sufficient evidence of lean production being successfully applied, both in its country of origin – Japan – and the UK (see the Ambi-Rad example below). There are, however, many cases where a system of lean production has failed to bring the expected benefits (as can be seen in Sherlock Security example below). There do, however, seem to be some clear indicators as to when lean production is likely to work and the circumstances in which it could be likely to fail.

Contrasting experiences of lean production

Ambi-Rad

Ambi-Rad, an engineering company in the Midlands, was a 'traditional' UK business for many years. In 1998, conditions were less than favourable. Engineering was generally seen as being in decline in the UK, and the strong pound was making it very difficult to compete in any international market.

The founder and co-owner of the business, Mike Brookes, initiated a fundamental change in the culture of the business, leading to a lean production system. In particular, team leaders were given the task of facilitating the generation of new ideas by the shop-floor workforce and bringing about their adoption by senior managers.

The key gains have been in terms of employee motivation, with workers saying they feel much more involved in the firm, and in keeping costs down. It is believed that suggestions from the shop floor have led to cost savings of £300,000, allowing the firm to both increase its sales and maintain its profit margins, despite the adverse trading conditions. The aim is to raise savings from the new system to at least £500,000 every year.

(Source: *Financial Times* 23 November 1999)

Sherlock Security Systems Ltd

When the doors closed for the final time at Sherlock Security Systems Ltd., set up 10 years earlier, the company had seen its operations expand from its local base to coverage of the North of England and North Wales. However, competition was intense and, in response to a decline in results in 1997, the firm attempted to remodel the company along the lines suggested by business gurus to take advantages of the benefits of a lean production system.

The expected cost savings and worker participation never materialised. Indeed, the changes imposed by the senior managers appear to have caused more problems than they actually solved. Workers resented the idea that the future of the business rested with them and their ability to make improvements to the firm's production systems. Workers also felt that their ideas were not fully welcomed by middle

FACT FILE

Lean production can trace its roots to the Toyota company in post-war Japan. Mass production was riddled with inflexibility and waste, and so a system was devised to allow production processes to be as flexible and efficient as possible. For example, to adjust a machine from producing one component to another in a large US firm took a whole day, and required the input of specialist engineers. The Toyota system ultimately reduced this time to three minutes, and the task could be carried out by production-line workers.

FACT FILE

The leading book on lean producton is *The Machine that Changed the World*, which was the result of a $5 million worldwide study into auto production organised by the Massachusetts Institute of Technology (MIT). The study showed that the best Japanese companies could produce with 'half the amount' of inputs required by North American or European producers.

managers, who already felt overburdened in their roles. They had seen the company expand, only to find their own workload increasing at the same rate.

The ultimate decline of the business was due to more than the misapplication of a lean production system. Perhaps the intended benefits could have helped the firm through its competitive difficulties and kept it going, if other problems had not compounded to prevent success.

Lean production is more likely to be successful if:

■ *The talents of all workers are positively encouraged* – as described by the motivation theories of Mayo and Herzberg, workers need to feel that they have a stake in the fortunes of the business. By using a stakeholder approach, managers encourage workers to give their best efforts to the business. Motivation can be achieved by schemes such as profit sharing and share ownership, and by managers adopting a personal touch.

■ *Quality assurance is built in, and is not a bolt-on extra* – having the quality of work checked by an inspector at the end of a production line is expensive in two ways. Firstly, of course, there is the wage and other costs directly associated with the team of inspectors. In addition, if defects are found, the whole item may have to be returned along the production chain and the work will have to be done again. In an extreme case, the whole item may be scrapped. A lean production system would encourage all workers to ensure that their work is done correctly before the piece is passed to the next internal customer on the production line. Mistakes are rectified sooner and there is no need for expensive checking at the end of the process.

■ *There are clear lines of communication* – one key component of a lean production system is the ability of all members of staff to communicate efficiently and effectively with any other member of staff. Channels of communication should be clear to all and there should be adequate provision for feedback to take place. In addition, there ought to be a corporate culture that fully supports openness between all levels of the business. Communication channels will only work successfully if each member of staff is committed to their use.

■ *The market is price sensitive* – the most important way in which lean production aids the competitiveness of a business is by reducing the overall costs of the business, allowing them to compete by reducing price whilst maintaining an adequate profit margin. Of course, if demand for a product is price inelastic, the potential for reducing price will not be advantageous – a price reduction will not attract a significant number of new customers.

■ *The market demands regular product improvements* – another key contribution that lean production can make to competitiveness is in its ability to modify and up-date products quickly, to keep pace with changing consumer demand. A car manufacturer needs to be able to adapt to new ideas and trends relatively quickly, and so would benefit from the degree of flexibility built in to lean production techniques.

■ *Any change is carefully managed* – the introduction of any new way of working, whether it be lean production or another system, implies a degree of change taking place throughout the organisation. Human nature can make staff at all levels reluctant to embrace new ideas, preferring instead to keep to tried and familiar methods. The imposition of sudden change may not always produce the intended results, especially if met with resistance from the workforce. As shall be seen later in this chapter, there are techniques that may be applied to allow change to be implemented smoothly.

There are, though, circumstances in which lean production is unlikely to lead to improvements for a firm. If one or more of the above criteria are absent, the firm may not benefit from the potential of a lean production system. In addition, lean production may not be successful when there is:

- *An inappropriate set of demands on the workforce* – there will be many workers at all levels in businesses who find the demands of a lean production system at odds with their abilities and expectations. This may be the case if, for example, compulsory targets are set for the number of suggestions that each worker has to put forward in a year. This could lead to an increase in the stress on the workforce and a consequent decrease in workers' morale and motivation.

- *A lack of motivation in the workforce* – motivation comes from many sources. In the real world there are many examples of workers who give less than their best in their workplace. Where a business has been less than successful in the past at motivating the workforce, an attempt to introduce a system of lean production is likely to face severe opposition and a negative reaction. Without the co-operation of the workforce it would be extremely difficult, if not impossible, to make the necessary changes in an appropriate way.

- *A lack of belief by senior and middle managers* – the philosophy of lean production must permeate the whole business. If any level of the business hierarchy fails to accept the system, it will cause severe blockages in the flow of communications and information. The flexibility required may be affected.

- *A static, long-established market place* – although it is an accepted fact of business life that change is inevitable, there can be a wide variety in the rate of change in different markets. How regularly, for example, do building materials change compared to computer technology? A slower rate of change means that firms do not require the degree of flexibility associated with lean production.

- *A poor presentation of the ideas in the initial stages* – lean production has come to be associated with the rationalisation of the workplace and its possible redundancies. Fear or scepticism would be a common reaction, especially if there is a lack of trust between different levels of the firm, as well as weak communications.

KEY POINTS

The need for lean production is likely to be greater if:

- competitors have adopted such techniques
- the market is price sensitive
- the firm is presently uncompetitive.

KEY POINTS

Lean production is less likely to work if:

- the culture of the organisation is autocratic
- the management is not committed to change
- employees resist change.

PROGRESS CHECK

Discuss whether lean production is appropriate for all firms in all situations.

KEY POINTS

The introduction of lean production techniques will be easier if:

- employees are suitably rewarded
- the need for change is explained to the employees
- if employees can see that it will work
- jobs are not lost.

The management of change

The introduction of a lean production system will, as noted previously, necessitate change within the business. As with any change, careful management of the process is important if the changes introduced are to be successful.

Although it is the production system that is being changed by the introduction of lean production techniques, the key to the successful management of the change is the handling and involvement of the *people* in the business.

Individuals may resist change if they perceive it as a threat to their status, their work group, their pay or even their continued employment at the firm. Very often, the problems of change are exaggerated by a lack of communication from those proposing and implementing the change. Some people have a natural tendency to look on the pessimistic side of life. If there is a lack of information and gossip begins to circulate within the firm, people imagine the worst-case scenario. This can get quite out of proportion as rumours escalate.

The key to managing the introduction of lean production, then, lies in staff involvement, since everyone will be affected by the changes. Everyone must be kept informed of the changes at each stage of the process, and the chance to have questions answered through two-way communications will help to overcome the possible negative effects of the grapevine.

PROGRESS CHECK

Discuss possible reasons why employees might resist the introduction of lean production.

KEY TERM

Business guru
a writer on business who presents ideas on the 'right' way to manage companies successfully. They are usually academics presenting the results of research into businesses, or practising managers passing on the wisdom of their experiences. Examples include: Ansoff, Deming, Drucker, Handy, Harvey Jones, Peters and Porter.

The future of lean production – trend or fad?

One characteristic of business management in the second half of the twentieth century was the development of the 'ultimate solution' to the question of how to run a business. A succession of business 'gurus' put forward models that became 'flavour of the month' – until their limitations were recognised and the theory was surpassed by the next 'big idea'.

So, does lean production fit into the same category of ideas that will come and go, or does it genuinely offer something that can be applied to many business situations? At the present time, there is an increasing quantity of compelling evidence suggesting that, when implemented appropriately, the system can provide firms with an increased degree of competitiveness in terms of both cost savings and improved flexibility.

Firms, large and small, from industrial giants such as Ford in the United States to regional concerns across the UK, are successfully adapting the techniques of lean production to suit their own circumstances.

The increasing degree of competition being faced by firms in Europe, thanks in part to the increasing economic harmonisation resulting from the European Union and its single currency, means that firms have to exploit what competitive advantages they can. In addition, many firms selling in consumer markets are finding that increasing wealth is creating more fickle consumers who demand constant change and a supply of up-to-the-minute products. This is particularly true in any area which is touched by high technology, where regular improvements are being made in the quality and performance of products. It is these sorts of challenges that lean production seems best equipped to deal with. It seems likely that the philosophy encapsulated by lean production will survive and prosper well into the twenty-first century.

PROGRESS CHECK

Discuss the factors which may determine whether lean production is a fad.

Summary chart

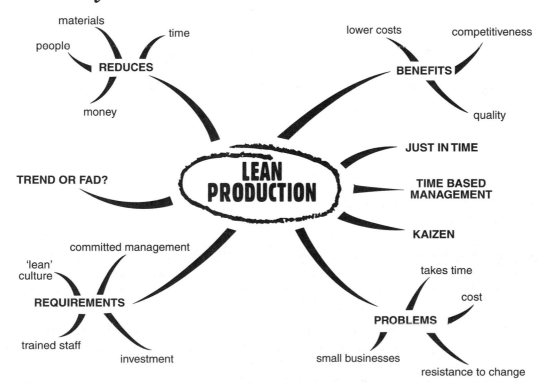

Figure 5.1 Lean production

Approaching exam questions: lean production

Examine three possible indicators of a successful lean production system.

(9 marks)

A good answer to a question like this clearly sets out the three points the student wishes to make. There is no need for detailed extended writing or setting out the answer as a single whole. It is a good technique to separate each point into different paragraphs and to number each point raised. This way the examiner can clearly see that three points have been made and can judge each one on its merits, rather than having to hunt through a single mass of words attempting to find out if three ideas have been given.

Should you include more than three points? When working under exam conditions, the time constraints mean that, usually, you shouldn't. However, if a fourth point comes readily to mind and can be included in a couple of sentences, it may be worthwhile adding it, just in case the examiner doesn't agree with one of the other points or feels that some of the points are repetitions. Examiners will mark any point made, and credit will be given to the best three (*not* the first three). Apart from the time issue, there is no penalty for making more points than are asked for in the question.

Points that could be raised in the context of indicators of successful lean production are:

- a general reduction in the firm's average costs
- an improvement in the quality record of the firm's products
- a greater ability to compete
- survival in difficult circumstances
- the achievement, or at least a movement towards, benchmarked standards.

Assess the possible contribution of lean production to the motivation of the workforce.

(11 marks)

In order to give an answer to this type of question, it would be worthwhile adopting one of the better-known motivational theories as a basis. Perhaps the most appropriate model for this type of question would be Herzberg's two-factor theory, although both Maslow's Hierarchy of Needs and Mayo's Hawthorne Effect could be used (see *People and Organisations* (ISBN: 0340 77231 X) in this series).

The key to achieving high marks lies in using the chosen theory as a means of assessing the contribution of lean production to motivation. Taking Herzberg's two-factor theory, it could be argued that achievement, recognition and responsibility, all motivators according to Herzberg, are likely to be enhanced by lean production. Similarly, lean production may help develop hygiene factors, such as relationships with supervisors and peers, and status so that they do not act as de-motivators.

Analyse the possible implications of being the first company to market a new product idea.

(11 marks)

When faced with a question asking for a consideration of implications, the answer should usually put forward both sides of a two-sided argument. Too often students see business questions in black and white – something is either a good thing or bad. In reality, good and bad points go hand-in-hand so that the elusive skill of evaluation needs to be brought into play.

In this case, the positive effects of being first out with a new product could be:

- market skimming
- brand loyalties can develop
- the firm's reputation may be enhanced.

On the other hand, it can bring problems such as:

- the firm has to sort out all the technical details and resolve problems that other firms can learn from
- the marketing costs, especially if the product relies on a completely new concept, are likely to be high
- later models from competitors can build on the groundwork done and refine the features in line with the experience of consumer demands.

Discuss the possible importance of communications channels to a lean production system.

(40 marks)

'Discussion' questions also require a two-sided approach, leading to a conclusion based on the preceding arguments. When discussing the importance of a single factor, the logical approach is to look firstly at the reasons why it is important, then to give some consideration to the other factors that are also be important to the success of lean production. A balanced conclusion may well conclude that communication is important to the system, but that it is only one significant factor. A good communication system by itself would not be sufficient to ensure the successful implementation of lean production.

The reasons why communication is important could include:

- the need for suggestions to move from the shop floor upward
- the requirement for adequate feedback
- workers' need for a feeling of belonging.

Other crucial factors could include:

- flexibility
- leadership style
- the external market.

Student answers

Assess the importance of a firm being flexible in a rapidly changing market

(9 marks)

Student answer

Flexibility is the way a firm can quickly change its products or services. It is important because of the dynamic business environment. Competitors will be bringing out new products and customers want the latest things. If the market is changing rapidly, the firm must be able to keep up with the changes and so will have to be able to launch new products on a regular basis.

Marker's comments

This answer has the makings of a good response, but ultimately it is apparent that the student has only a vague notion of the importance of flexibility. The answer repeats the same point twice.

There has been little attempt to answer the actual question. The key word is 'assess': there has been no attempt at assessment, rather there is a generalised statement.

How important is flexibility? Are any other factors as, or even more, important? What would the consequences be of a lack of flexibility? These are possible issues that could be covered to address this question.

Mark: Content 2/2, Application 1/4, Analysis 0/3. Total = 3

Outline the problems a firm might face in introducing lean production.

(9 marks)

Student answer

Despite the benefits that a firm may get from lean production, there may be problems in its introduction. These could be:

- Resistance from the workforce. Lean production often means that some workers are made redundant. The fear of this could make the workforce reluctant to take part in the process of introducing lean production. If the workers refuse to get involved, one of the key aspects of lean production, the involvement of all personnel, cannot be achieved.

- The need to change the firm's internal structures. The changes needed in terms of communications channels, work practices, and roles and responsibilities could all be poorly implemented, or even not considered at all. Such errors would seriously undermine the chances of the lean production initiative being successful.

Marker's comments

This is a fair attempt. The structure is clear, and each point is outlined as required by the question. The first point in particular is well developed and explained.

Mark: Content 2/2, Application, 3/4, Analysis 2/3. Total = 7

Analyse the reasons why some firms may fail to adopt lean production techniques.

(9 marks)

Student answer

1 Lack of knowledge. Some managers may be too busy to learn about new techniques such as lean production. They may have studied business before the ideas became popular and so have only a limited understanding of it. However, it ought to be a duty of managers to keep themselves aware of developments in the business environment. So, this is really a fault that shouldn't happen if managers are doing their job properly.
2 Not believing lean production works. Managers may be aware of lean production but may think it is only a passing fad, or may have heard of companies where the idea has been tried and it hasn't worked. If this happens they will be very reluctant to take the chance of using it themselves.
3 The idea is not always appropriate to every firm in every circumstance. In slow markets, for example, firms may rely on their traditional way of doing things and will not be facing much change outside the business to prompt them to change inside.

Marker's comments

A thorough answer which deals with both the content required by the question, as well as its instruction to 'analyse'.

Mark: Content 2/2, Application 4/4, Analysis 3/3. Total = 9

Evaluate the possible impact on a workforce of introducing lean production.

(11 marks)

Student answer

Workers will be happy at the introduction of lean production since it allows them a greater say in the running of the business. They can make suggestions that managers must adopt and this will increase the workers' self-esteem. The jobs people do will be more interesting and exciting, and will increase their motivation.

Lean production is a good thing for workers.

Marker's comments

The candidate has failed to recognise that this is a two-sided question. The impact will be both positive and negative. The negative side has been missed completely (e.g. redundancies). The positive side has been wildly exaggerated by the use of sweeping generalisations.

Although this candidate has some relevant notions, little use is made of them here.

Mark: Content 1/2, Application & Analysis 2/6, Evaluation 0/3. Total = 3

End of section questions

1 In what sense is lean production a philosophy rather than a way of working?

(9 marks)

2 Consider the possible advantages of a lean production system.

(9 marks)

3 Discuss the extent to which adopting lean production is inevitable for any business.

(11 marks)

4 Examine the circumstances in which the introduction of lean production may **not** be successful.

(9 marks)

5 Consider the impact lean production could have for the UK economy if it were to be adopted by large numbers of UK firms.

(9 marks)

6 Analyse the possible implications for a firm if competitors adopt a lean production system.

(11 marks)

7 To what extent can lean production be considered a 'fad'?

(11 marks)

8 Discuss the case for lean production from the perspective of the personnel department.

(11 marks)

9 Assess whether lean production is likely to be viable for a small-scale producer.

(11 marks)

10 Discuss the potential problems of introducing a lean production system.

(11 marks)

Essays

1 Can lean production be successfully introduced in all manufacturing businesses?

(40 marks)

2 To what extent is lean production a guarantee of success?

40 marks)

3 Evaluate the potential benefits of introducing lean production for a medium-sized producer of components for the motor industry.

(40 marks)

4 To what extent do you agree that lean production is a 'philosophy rather than a tool box of measures'?

(40 marks)

5 'The introduction of lean production is simply a way of making redundancies'. Discuss this statement.

(40 marks)

CHAPTER 6

Research and Development, and innovation

Introduction

Research and Development involves developing new products and processes (i.e. it examines both *what* is made and *how* it is made). R&D is followed by **innovation** which is the exploitation of these new ideas. The two elements of research and development, and innovation combine to turn an idea into an actual product or service that is ready for the marketplace. By innovating firms can provide better quality goods and services in new ways; they can cut costs, improve quality and widen their product offerings. Innovation allows firms to develop new markets, to have their own unique selling proposition (USP) and to gain a competitve advantage over their rivals. According to the Department of Trade and Industry's report on UK business 'Winning companies are focused on all aspects of the business that will enable them to exploit new ideas successfully, whether in the production process ... or in after sales service, ... Winning companies constantly exceed their customers' expectation with new products and services'.

KEY TERMS

Research and development
developing promising ideas into workable propositions.

Innovation
turning the results of research and development into a commercial reality.

> **Research and development is the driver of innovation; innovation is the driver of progress.**

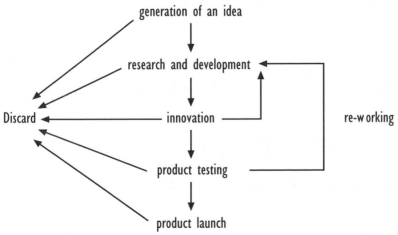

Figure 6.1 Developing a new product

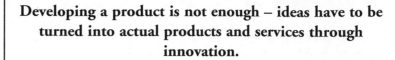

Developing a product is not enough – ideas have to be turned into actual products and services through innovation.

Not every idea can be successful. There will be many occasions on which ideas are disregarded totally if no further progress is likely. Often the process returns to an earlier stage for further developmental work in the light of problems being uncovered.

Stages of product development

New ideas

Completely 'new' products are very rare. Most new products are developments of already existing ones. The most likely sources of new product ideas are the firm's own products, other firms' products, customers, staff, product research, and rumours of the developments being made by other firms.

Research and Development

Research helps to uncover new ideas about products, methods of production, materials technology and so on. The development aspect aids the progression of ideas and also acts as a filter, allowing the firm to concentrate on those ideas that seem most likely to be successful.

Innovation

Innovation has been described as the point at which new product development meets reality. Up to this point, the reality of a new product launch can be set to one side in favour of following an interesting idea to see where it leads. Innovation must take account of the realities of the process, such as production costs, potential selling prices and demand for the product, the position of competitors and so on.

Product testing

Once an idea has been finalised and developed, the resulting product will be tested for both its performance and the impression it makes on potential customers. Problems are likely to be identified at this stage, allowing the firm to return to the development stage to improve and modify the product.

Product launch

Once the firm is happy with the results of the process, it is in a position to launch its new product. In the real world, there may be enormous pressure to launch new products to match the actions of competitors or to boost the falling performance of existing products. This can mean that products are released before they have been fully developed, leading to problems in the future. Products that have been launched can be protected through patents and trademarks.

PROGRESS CHECK

Analyse the factors which are likely to lead to the successful development of a new product idea.

The importance of Research and Development

Research and Development is an important aspect of a firm's competitive strategy. If a business stands still for any length of time, it will find that it has been overtaken by its competitors. The last 20 years of the twentieth century were witness to an increasingly rapid pace of change in terms of the development of new products. Consumers are now seen as being less loyal and more demanding of continuous improvements and change. Firms must react to this by developing new products for their customers and by finding new ways of serving their needs. The explosion of e-commerce (trade via the Internet) in recent years highlights how innovative organisations are always seeking to find new ways of meeting their customer needs.

Innovation is particularly important in an international marketplace. Developing products for a variety of different markets requires a commitment to a differentiated approach, with an investment of resources and time.

PROGRESS CHECK

Is it possible for a firm to prosper without some commitment to Research and Development? If not, why not? If so, how? Would you recommend such a strategy?

R&D investment

There is no clear correlation between spending time and money on Research and Development, and the creation of successful products. Simply spending more money does not guarantee that a firm will come up with more successful ideas. There is, therefore, no guarantee that the creative process of R&D ultimately results in a product that meets the needs of consumers. This can make budgeting for research and development quite difficult. How much should or could a company spend if there is no guarantee of a return on the investment? However, there are factors that can be considered which make success more likely:

■ the needs of customers

FACT FILE

Patents remain the most important form of protection of intellectual property (ideas) with 61% of manufacturers and 37% of non-manufacturers filing patents in 1997.

FACT FILE

- The catseye, used to mark the centre of roads, was patented in March 1935 and has since earned over £3 million.
- The ring pull (used on cans) was patented in June 1965 and has earned over £50 m.
- The Polaroid was patented in June 1946 and has earned over $650 m.

- the firm's strengths
- the competition
- the market.

Considering the needs of consumers

The reason that firms have a marketing function is to help them meet the needs of their consumers. It follows that, if a firm is attempting seriously to develop successful products or services, it must take account of the demands of potential consumers. Whilst there may be limitations on the usefulness of marketing research, the results do present a firm with a starting point from which they can proceed.

There will, however, be occasions when a significant research breakthrough presents the opportunity to provide consumers with something beyond their current requirements. This is often seen in technological areas. The vast majority of consumers are more than happy with their current VCR system. Technological developments, however, have led to the development of the DVD system and a whole new range of products is becoming available. In effect, a demand has been created based on the results of Research and Development.

Considering the strengths of the firm

Market research findings are not sufficient by themselves to guide a firm's developmental activities. Each firm has its own assets and strengths which ought to be exploited if the business is to create a clear advantage over its competitors. It would be uncompetitive for a firm to develop a product completely counter to its own strengths and the capabilities of its assets, just as the development of superior products is senseless if it goes against the requirements of the marketplace.

Taking account of strengths and assets is the basis of the asset-led approach. An example of this was the development of the Mars Bar into an ice-cream. The firm started with the assets of an existing product, its brand name and its reputation, and developed this to enter the 'luxury' ice-cream market. This was being developed at the time by more traditional ice-cream manufacturers.

Considering the actions of competitors

One important source of new products is the competitive environment. In highly competitive markets, it is important to anticipate the developments being made by rivals, rather than waiting until their new products are on the market. Being the first to produce a new idea gives a firm a clear advantage in terms of developing brand loyalty and getting a foothold in the marketplace. However, not being first doesn't imply not bothering.

'Me-too' products are often important competitive weapons in a firm's product portfolio.

FACT FILE

Customer expectations and competition remain the main drivers of innovation for both manufacturing and non-manufacturing sectors.
Source: *CBI Innovation Trends Survey*

KEY TERM

An asset-led approach to developing new products is based on the firm's strengths, as well as taking account of the demand from consumers.

KEY TERM

A 'me-too' product is one that is new to a firm but is largely an imitation of a successful existing one from a different manufacturer.

Considering the likely state of the market

Research and Development is a long-term activity. Firms must attempt to consider how their marketplace will develop in the future. If the market is fashion-led, even quite short-term developments can be hard to predict. It would be a costly mistake to go ahead with the development of a product that is behind the times as soon as it is launched. Equally, if the economy seems to be heading for a recession, it is likely to be pointless to develop products for the luxury end of the market.

Modern approaches to Research and Development

Modern production techniques embodied in the 'Japanisation' of production favour an approach to product development called **simultaneous engineering**. This means organising the Research and Development function so that the different stages are carried out in conjunction, instead of in sequence. This reduces the time taken to get an idea to the marketplace, which cuts costs and provides an extra competitive advantage over other firms that may be taking a more linear approach to their product development. In order to implement simultaneous engineering, a firm has to ensure that its internal structures and culture are designed to support its operations. The most important aspects to be considered are:

KEY TERM

Simultaneous engineering is the co-ordination of the Research and Development function to allow the quicker launch of new ideas as finished products.

- providing improved communications, in terms of both speed and accuracy, between all the different functions of the business

- having an organisational structure that is flexible enough to allow the formation of project teams from the different functions of the business (such as Research and Development, marketing, finance, production)

- ensuring the processes are in place to allow the simultaneous development of the product, its production and the marketing processes – with all the functions working in tandem, all ought to be moving in the same direction.

PROGRESS CHECK

Assess the likely problems of adopting a system of simultaneous engineering.

The risks of Research and Development

In spite of the importance attached to Research and Development, there is a degree of risk attached as well. There can be a high cost associated with the development of new products or processes, and there is never a guaranteed return.

Given the potentially high cost of developing new products, firms find themselves in the difficult position of balancing the need for development against the potential cost of failing to develop successful products. The factors that make Research and Development more likely to be successful have been discussed (page 103–105). Set against these must be the costs of such research efforts. The costs to be considered include:

■ *Staffing costs* – in forming a multi-disciplinary research team, as advocated by the simultaneous engineering approach, the firm will be taking people out of their normal function area. Their salaries must be met, as will the pay of replacement workers, until such time as the flexible team is disbanded and the staff return to their original positions.

■ *Capital costs* – development teams are likely to require access to capital equipment, which is made temporarily unavailable for the 'normal' production function. In addition, it is likely that the team will investigate the capabilities of the latest technologies and their potential application to the business. This could lead to recommendations for heavy investment.

■ *Materials* – in a similar way, the team may need access to materials, both those currently used within the business and potential alternatives that may need to be more fully investigated for their properties and applications.

■ *Time* – although not normally given a specific cost in monetary terms, the time spent on a research project inevitably detracts from the time available for the running of the 'proper' business.

FACT FILE

Glaxo-SmithKline, the giant pharmaceutical company, spends nearly $4 billion on research and development a year; this accounts for a fifth of all UK research spending!

KEY POINTS

A firm is more likely to undertake Research and Development if:

- the rate of technological change in its industry is rapid
- the firm has a clear competitive advantage that it wishes to protect
- another firm in the industry has a clear competitive advantage that can be challenged
- the firm takes a long-term view of its ability to compete
- the government provides financial incentives.

PROGRESS CHECK

Discuss whether or not it would be possible for a firm to undertake a Cost/Benefit analysis for its research and development function.

Research and Development in different markets

Of course, not all businesses are in markets where there is a persistent need for change. In some areas the pace of change is less rapid than in others. However, even in slower moving markets it is always a mistake to assume that there is no need for research and development. Complacency is often a causal factor when long-established market leaders are overtaken by other firms who have developed new ideas or responded to new opportunities arising in the marketplace.

There are types of markets where research and development is more necessary or more urgent than in others. In the pharmaceutical industry, for example, the very survival of organisations depends on their ability to innovate; once a product is successful and patented, it gives the firm security for a few years. But the patent will end at some point and competitors will launch similar products, so firms must keep investing to innovate. In general, the characteristics of markets in which spending on Research and Development is high include:

■ *A dependence on technology* –there has been rapid development of technology over recent decades. Firms who rely on technology, whether for their production process or the actual product, need to develop their approach to keep up with competitors.

■ *Speed of change within the marketplace* – in a fast-moving market, it is important that firms are always thinking ahead to the next bestseller. A past reputation in fashion clothing or the music industry is unlikely to help if the latest 'in-thing' is something completely different.

■ *A high degree of competition* – if a firm is facing stiff competition it needs every competitive advantage it can acquire. Research and Development is one way in which that vital extra edge can be gained.

■ *The existence of barriers to entry* – barriers to entry are those factors which allow a firm to dominate a market by preventing other firms competing in an effective way. Often, these barriers are in the form of the market leader's cost advantages or consumer loyalty. Although such firms have a clear advantage, they are occasionally upstaged by smaller firms who develop new products or approaches that steal the market. A classic example was seen in the world of computers. During the 1960s and 1970s IBM had a clear advantage in terms of its size and presence in the market, the brand loyalty it had established and the cost advantages it had over any other firm entering the market. Its decline towards the end of the 1970s and into the 1980s is largely attributable to its failure to recognise and prepare for the changes in its market brought about by developments being made by other firms, such as Microsoft and Hewlett Packard.

Research and Development in the UK

Although research and development is important for individual businesses, it is also seen as important for the economic prosperity of the nation as a whole. Successive governments have encouraged businesses to invest in research as a means of maintaining the country's international competitiveness. In the pre-budget statement in November 1999 the Chancellor of the Exchequer, Gordon Brown, placed a heavy emphasis on the need for UK firms to be increasing their international competitiveness to enhance the country's economic prosperity.

Spending as a percentage of sales revenue

UK firms spend far less on Research and Development as a percentage of the sales revenue they earn than companies in other leading economies. Even amongst the top spenders on Research and Development within the UK there is a significant difference in the relative level as a percentage of total sales. For example, Glaxo Wellcome, the pharmaceuticals company which merged with SmithKline Beacham, had the highest absolute spending on research and development of over £1bn per year. This was around 15% of annual sales. Lower down the list, though, comes Shell Transport and Trading, the company which – despite having the fifth largest total spending on Research and Development at slightly under half a billion pounds – is actually only spending half of one per cent of its total sales revenue.

The UK and the rest of the World

In absolute terms, the UK spends an average 2.3% of sales revenue on Research and Development, less than 11 other major economies. The USA, for example, spends 4.3% of sales value on development, Germany 4.7% and Japan 4.9%. Given that these economies are much larger than the UK's, the *actual* level of spending is significantly more than twice the UK's spending. The countries with the highest proportionate spending on Research and Development are Canada, with 10.8%, and Denmark with 15.1%.

The implication is that UK firms are less likely to be able to compete effectively on the international stage in the future. Foreign companies may reap the benefits of their enhanced Research and Development spending, leaving UK firms to play 'catch-up'.

How much should a firm spend on R&D?

Spending on R&D is determined by how much the firm has got to spend overall. If a firm has not got the money (or cannot borrow it) it cannot spend it. The amount of spending is also affected by the expected returns. However, the problem with basing expenditure on the projected payback is that managers do not necessarily know how likely it is that a particular product or service will succeed. Even if it does sell well it is difficult to estimate just how successful it will be.

Spending levels also depend on the perceived need for research and spending by competitors. In industries such as washing powder and toothpaste, the constant development of new products forces all firms which want to remain competitive to spend heavily on innovation.

Why do UK firms tend to spend less?

The short-term view

Part of the problem may be that UK firms tend to take a short-term view. Research and Development expenditure requires a commitment to the long term. Innovation takes time to happen. In the UK, many investors are financial institutions which look for short-term rewards; as a result these shareholders are less likely to allow managers to invest in research.

Culture

Another reason for the low levels of investment may be that UK firms lack an innovative culture. To encourage innovation, people have to be able to fail – when trying something new there will almost inevitably be problems. Mistakes will be made and some ideas will fail. Managers seeking innovation must not criticise such failure but accept that it is a necessary part of the innovative process. Only if people feel able to fail will they try in the first place. Organisations in Silicon Valley, for example, have a tremendous reputation for allowing people to be creative, to try things out and to attempt to develop products or services even if they seem far-fetched. By comparison, a bureaucratic organisation which rewards only those who do as they are told is less likely to be innovative.

The degree of innovation within a business may also be related to the expectations of management. Companies such as 3M set clear targets for new product development in terms of the percentage of revenue that it wants generated by new products, and actively encourage and support experimentation. This acts as a focus for innovative activity.

Competition

The extent to which firms invest in Research and Development also depends on the degree of competition in the industry. The more competition there is, the more likely it is that a firm will strive to innovate in order to remain competitive. Compared to, say, the USA many markets in the UK are not particularly competitive and this removes some of the pressure to improve.

> **Competition forces innovation.**

Finance

UK firms may be held back by the difficuties and expense of getting finance for Research and Development. Although the government is certainly very interested in innovation within the economy, it has been criticised for failing to provide enough tax concessions and grants. Also, the relatively high interest rates and cautious lending policies of financial institutions are said to have constrained UK firms' innovation.

Should the government spend more on innovation?

Innovation is a dynamic force within the economy. It creates new products and new ways of doing things. Firms which innovate are more likely to anticipate customers' needs and develop a competitive advantage. This can create wealth and jobs. Governments should, therefore, be very concerned about the level of innovation in the economy. It might be argued that governments should spend more on innovation, either directly through investment in its own programmes or via grants to private sector firms. Whilst this may be desirable, governments do have all kinds of different demands on their spending and innovation may not be seen as the priority. Also, there is the problem that simply spending more does not guarantee more innovation – it may just lead to more failed ideas. Furthermore, how good is the government likely to be at picking winning products and winning companies? Who would judge success?

Rather than increase spending on Research and Development, UK governments have been eager to bring together financiers and ideas people so that they can

FACT FILE

'The challenge for the UK is to create a business culture in which innovation becomes an everyday activity though which people in businesses large and small seek new ideas from a wide range of sources and have the expertise, flair and courage to exploit them effectively.' Peter Mandelson DTI 1998

FACT FILE

At 3M employees are allowed to use part of their annual budget on whatever they want; the idea is that this encourages people to develop their own ideas.

FACT FILE

Retained profit is the most important source of finance for innovation, accounting for about 85% of manufacturers' and 77% of non-manufacturers' spending in this area.

FACT FILE

In the 1990s Trevor Bayliss developed a clockwork radio for use in less developed countries where the electricity supply was limited and access to batteries not practical. He had enormous trouble getting financial backing for a product that has since been highly successful.

arrange their own projects. Simply bringing together people with ideas for new ventures and those with money can stimulate innovation. Government strategy has focused on helping information to flow between firms, between entrepreneurs, between universities and other research departments in the belief that this networking will stimulate better exploitation of ideas within the UK.

Certainly, spending more is not necessarily the key; the important thing is how the money is used to generate more ideas and to enable these ideas to be turned into actual products and services. As ever, it is not the *amount* of spending but the *quality* of the spending – is it targetted in the right areas? It may only be possible to judge the success of the approach adopted by recent UK goverments in the future when the ideas have or have not led to successful products and services in the marketplace.

Summary chart

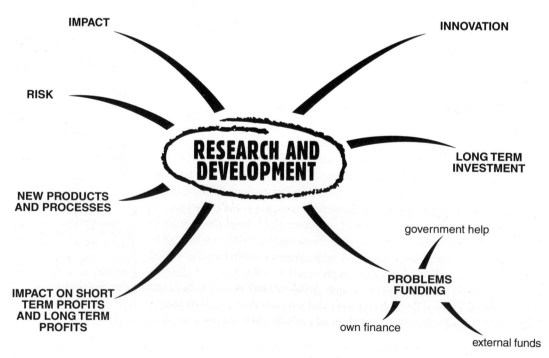

Figure 6.2 Research and development

Approaching exam questions: Research and Development, and innovation

Outline the likely features of an effective Research and Development team.

(9 marks)

A question which asks for factors to be outlined does not require a detailed discussion of each point raised, although the key features should be explained in the general context of the question.

A common issue raised by students is how many features each question requires. When the question is plural, as in this case, at least two points should be covered. Remember, though, that examiners are interested in much more than knowledge of the syllabus area. Equally important are skills such as selectivity and application. If the candidate raises too many different points, it is unlikely that he or she will also be able to demonstrate these higher level skills. The general rule of thumb, then, would be to cover two or possibly three different points, or as many are asked for in the question.

For this question, possible features of an R&D team that could be introduced are:

■ team members should come from different areas of the business

■ membership should be flexible so that it can be altered at will

■ the team's work must be fully supported by the culture of the business

■ the team must be given access to all necessary resources.

To gain good marks students would have to explain each point in terms of its contribution to the effectiveness of the development process.

Discuss the importance of Research and Development to a firm in a hi-tec industry.

(11 marks)

This is a discussion question which requires a two-sided approach, and a suitable conclusion. Questions like this are often addressed in a simplistic, one-sided way, with candidates making several points stressing (or over-stressing) the importance of the issue. Students must attempt to place the issue in a balanced context.

Whilst Research and Development is important to firms, especially to those in a hi-tec industry, it is certainly not the *sole* determinant of business success. A balanced discussion would give a sense of proportion by placing this specific issue in the context of all the other features that can help a business to succeed.

On one side of the discussion, then, the candidate could raise such points as:

- competitors will probably be pushing ahead with new ideas on a regular basis
- consumers will often pay high prices for the latest innovations
- brand loyalty is very difficult to sustain in such markets.

On the other hand, the candidate can point to other factors that aid success such as:

- image
- reliability
- after sales service
- the ability of the firm to match Research and Development to customer needs.

Should a firm have a separate Research and Development department?

(11 marks)

A question like this can be approached by defining the exact meaning of the terms before moving on to an answer. In any case, it is a good idea to state the assumptions on which the answer is based. Does the question here mean a completely separate Research and Development department which operates independently from the rest of the business? Or does it mean a separate body that directs the Research and Development activities but that can draw on the resources and personnel of the whole business. Clearly, which assumption is made has a direct bearing on the answer that is constructed.

A completely separate R&D department may not draw on the expertise of the whole firm or its assets, and could easily head in a different direction to the rest of the organisation.

On the other hand, a body which directs the Research and Development function whilst drawing on the other areas of the firm is more likely to be integrated into the the business and will be more in line with its objectives. This kind of department is more likely to bring success to the firm. It must be noted, however, that there can be no guarantees in either case that the research and development will be successful.

Evaluate the arguments for and against government intervention in private firms' Research and Development.

(11 marks)

Any evaluation question requires the development of at least two different points of view, leading to an ultimate conclusion. In this case, the candidate is clearly required to raise at least one argument on either side. More than two points would probably cause the candidate to write too much in terms of content and not have enough time to develop the argument, demonstrating the higher level skills of analysis and evaluation.

Arguments for government intervention could include:

- the general economic prosperity of the country in terms of international trade, levels of employment, etc.
- the provision of aid may allow private firms to compete more effectively with larger international rivals

- a relatively small investment can bring large rewards directly to the government in terms of tax revenue.

Arguments against could include:

- since the amount a government could give would be finite, who would decide which firms benefit and which do not
- any government intervention distorts free competition
- if one government supports individual firms in this way, other countries could follow suit, leading to no real benefit for the first country.

On balance, then, such a policy could be useful, but only if it is carefully targeted.

Student answers

Outline the possible characteristics of markets in which Research and Development may be crucial to a firm's success.

(9 marks)

Student answer

Research and Development will be crucial to a firm which has a lot of hi-tec equipment. Since such equipment is being improved on an almost daily basis, a firm that doesn't keep up-to-date will certainly fall behind its competitors. Similarly, when a market has a high level of competition one means of getting ahead of rival firms could be to develop new products that meet the changing needs of consumers. Again, if a firm does not find some way of developing its products, it will find itself at a competitive disadvantage.

Marker's comments

Although short, this answer has some high quality features. The candidate has rightly limited the answer to a couple of points – any more and the answer would just repeat the demonstration of the required skill levels. Both points are effectively applied to the actual terms of the question and potential consequences are raised to score analysis marks.

Mark: Content 2/2, Application 3/4, Analysis 2/3. Total = 7

Consider the factors that might determine the extent to which a firm ought to invest in developing new products.

(11 marks)

Student answer

Investing in the development of new products is very important for a firm if it is to compete effectively in its market. The cost involved will be regained by the sales and profits from the new ideas when they are turned into new products. If a firm does not invest in new products it is likely to lose its customers to other firms.

Marker's comments

Although the candidate is making valid points about research and development, they are not directed at the question. The candidate has raised relevant points (potential returns and competitors) and so scores for content. However, they are not applied to this particular question and so there can be no reward for the higher level skills.

Mark: Content 2/2, Application & Analysis 0/6, Evaluation 0/3. Total = 2

Examine the reasons why the government might attempt to promote spending on Research and Development by UK firms.

(9 marks)

Student answer

There are several reasons why a government would want firms to spend more money on Research and Development. As part of the government's attempt to manage the domestic economy, it is concerned that UK firms can compete with foreign firms. One way to do this is to encourage R&D spending so that firms remain competitive, enhancing UK exports, reducing the need for imports and so improving the UK's balance of payments.

In addition, there are several areas of the UK that are suffering from high levels of unemployment. By encouraging investment in new technologies, the government, through grants etc., can encourage firms to locate in such areas, improving the standards of living for people who live there.

Without government intervention, it is doubtful whether firms would spend as much on R&D as they do at present.

Marker's comments

This answer starts very well. The first paragraph is excellent in its content and its direction. There is also good analysis.

Mark: Content 2/2, Application 4/4, Analysis 2/3. Total = 8

To what extent does Research and Development determine a firm's competitiveness?

(11 marks)

Student answer

Research and Development is an important element in some firm's competitiveness. If firms are in a dynamic market, they have to do everything they possibly can to keep up with developments and to have the product range necessary to compete with rivals. A firm that does not deploy its resources in the field of Research and Development may well fall behind its competitors and find its customers going elsewhere.

However, this does not apply to all firms in all circumstances. There are many other ways for firms to compete (such as using brand image, price and promotions). It is possible for a firm to compete effectively with 'me-too' products that require little in the way of detailed Research and Development.

Therefore, although Research and Development can be important to a firm's competitiveness, it is not the only factor to be considered. Different firms in different circumstances will place a different emphasis on Research and Development.

Marker's comments

This is a very well structured answer that clearly gives both sides of the argument before arriving at an appropriate conclusion. Each point is clearly explained in terms that are relevant to the question and well developed, albeit briefly. The only limitation of this answer is in the depth of analysis. Neither point is expanded to look at possible consequences to any great extent.

Mark: Content 2/2, Application & Analysis 4/6, Evaluation 2/3. Total = 8

End of section questions

1 Analyse the likely features of a strong Research and Development team.

(9 marks)

2 To what extent can a firm reduce the risks associated with Research and Development spending?

(9 marks)

3 Consider the possible long-term impact of a firm under-spending on Research and Development.

(9 marks)

4 Consider the possible benefits a process of simultaneous engineering can bring to a firm in a highly competitive market.

(9 marks)

5 Analyse the reasons why the government wishes to encourage more spending on Research and Development.

(9 marks)

6 Discuss the factors which might influence how much a firm spends on Research and Development.

(11 marks)

7 Discuss the possible risks involved in the process of Research and Development.

(11 marks)

8 Analyse the factors that may make investment in Research and Development more or less vital to the long-term survival of a firm.

(11 marks)

9 Evaluate the contribution of Research and Development to a firm's long-term success.

(11 marks)

10 'Copying other peoples' products is safer than waiting for your own inspiration.' Evaluate this statement.

(11 marks)

Essays

1 'Much of the spending on Research and Development leads to nothing, so firms should cut back rather than spend more.' Discuss.

(40 marks)

2 How far ought the government intervene to promote Research and Development by UK firms?

(40 marks)

3 'Paying for product development is a risk worth NOT worth taking.' Critically assess this view.

(40 marks)

4 How important is Research and Development for a firm in a service industry?

(40 marks)

5 Consider the circumstances in which a firm could survive without a significant investment in new product development.

(40 marks)

CHAPTER 7
Information technology

Introduction

Information Technology is the largest single growth area in modern business. It has developed so rapidly that many of the terms associated with recent developments are already in widespread use and are integral parts of everyday language. Consider the list below. Each term is in common usage, but very few, if any, were well known in the early 1990s:

- e-mail
- modem
- tele-working
- world wide web
- tele-conferencing
- hot-desking.

The explosion of Information Technology has inevitably led to some confusion and misconceptions. If you were to ask about the benefits of Information Technology, the answer may concentrate on the hardware involved (such as 'the use of computers') or on software applications (such as 'the programs that allow different functions to operate'). Alternatively, answers could concentrate on the communications aspects of e-mails, fax machines and so on, or on the ability to store and analyse large amounts of data. Clearly, each of these answers contains a part of the whole picture. The total answer goes much deeper than this.

The real benefit of Information Technology is that it provides a business with a competitive advantage, by allowing tasks to be carried out effectively, efficiently and cheaply. Different firms in different situations use different aspects of Information Technology to suit their own needs and to attempt to achieve their own goals. In other words, Information Technology centres around the integrated use of software, hardware and technological machinery to allow a firm to better achieve its organisational goals. By using Information Technology firms can acquire, analyse and distribute information more effectively. This allows managers to make better decisions, to understand problems and issues more fully and to react more quickly than competitors.

> **Information Technology is a tool which helps a business to achieve the organisation's goals.**

Is Information Technology always beneficial to a firm?

Establishing a competitive advantage through IT

A competitive advantage is a feature of a business that allows it to compete more effectively with other firms. Commonly identified competitive advantages lie in developing a Unique Selling Point for the firm's products or services, or being a lower cost producer.

Clearly, such advantages arise from a range of business activities such as promotions, the production processes or new product development. Nevertheless, there are several specific ways in which Information Technology can aid the development of a competitive advantage. These include:

■ *Improved efficiency* – the use of Information Technology can increase the productivity of a firm. Work can be carried out with a higher degree of accuracy and repetitive production tasks can be undertaken by robotics to give a more consistent level of work. In addition, IT can provide an increased level of support for workers and managers, in the form of up-to-date information and the ability to give quick, accurate analyses of the data.

■ *Improved quality* – the improved reliability of the production process and the use of accurate, up-to-date information allows the firm to reach higher general levels of quality. Output will be more reliable and more 'fit-for-purpose', and it ought to be possible to eliminate more inaccuracies than previously.

■ *New products* – the process of developing new products can be improved at all stages by the use of Information Technology. It is possible to gather quickly and analyse accurately market information to determine the actions of competitors, the responses of consumers and all the other factors that help to determine demand levels. This information ought to allow a firm to determine its next step in terms of new product development. The application of IT should also support the process of developing ideas from their initial concept all the way through to the launch of the product.

■ *After sales service* – even after a product has been launched, Information Technology can be applied to improve the level of after sales service, through keeping better data on customers, documenting the availability of spare parts, as well as providing customers with information specifically tailored to their needs and interests.

By itself, however, Information Technology is not sufficient to generate a competitive advantage. The new technology available to one firm is usually available to its competitors. In some ways, the move towards 'e-commerce' being made by many firms is a defensive one, rather than being the search for a competitive advantage. The fear is that, by *not* embracing such opportunities, a firm may be in danger of losing ground to its competitors.

KEY TERM

A competitive advantage is anything that allows one firm to attract more customers than others.

KEY POINTS

Information technology is more likely to be useful if:

● it reduces costs significantly
● it is managed effectively
● it provides the information which is needed for decision-makers at the right time and cost.

In what circumstances might the introduction of Information Technology *not* give a firm a competitive advantage?

At its best, Information Technology forms a key element of business success and helps maintain a firm's competitive position. However, this can only happen if IT is fully integrated with every other factor of the business. Information Technology must work in combination with the finance systems, the training systems, the organisational structure, and so on. Information Technology cannot aid the firm if it is seen as a stand-alone element of the business; something that has been bolted-on to the existing resources of the firm. Only by applying Information Technology in a coherent way can its potential benefits be made available to a firm.

Questions

Which of the following statements do you feel is the most accurate? Explain your answer.

Information technology will be:
a) the most important factor in a firm's development in the future
b) one of several important features in a firm's development in the future
c) of minor importance in a firm's development in the future.

> **The management of Information Technology is a strategic issue which contributes to business success or failure.**

The problems of Information Technology

Despite the clear potential benefits of Information Technology, it must be noted that its introduction brings potential problems as well. As with many business problems, difficulties can only be overcome if the problems are recognised and appropriate responses made.

The possible pitfalls are as follows.

Resistance to change

Employees are notoriously resistant to change. The introduction of new technology in particular may be seen as a threat to workers and their roles within a firm. At the

FACT FILE

IT creates new markets and new millionaires. Lastminute.com the Internet travel agent was floated in 2000 for over £700 million despite the fact it had never made a profit. Its founders, Martha Lane Fox and Brent Hoberman, were worth £45.5 million and £68 million respectively as a result.

FACT FILE

The five best performing sectors of 1999 in terms of returns for investors were:
1 telecommunications
2 Information Technology (hardware and software)
3 computer services
4 media
5 electronics.
All of these achieved returns of over 100%. The worst performing shares were in diversified industrials, food and drug retailers, insurance, food producers and water.

very least, employees may face a change to their status and their relationships at work. It may be that if managers adopt a Theory X attitude – that workers always resist change – any change is introduced in a defensive way creating a self-fulfilling prophecy. However, the broadening application of modern techniques of production and personnel management may develop a truly flexible workforce in the future; change will be more common, and workers and managers may be less prone to defensive reactions.

The need for training

Many aspects of new Information Technology require workers to develop new skills or update existing ones. For a proportion of the workforce acquiring these skills, linked with the perceived threat of new technology, will increase workers' stress levels and could contribute to sickness and absenteeism. At the very least, the firm will be faced with the cost of training its workers. As well as the direct costs of the training, the firm will also have to be aware of the indirect costs, such as the loss of output whilst employees are away from their normal work positions. On the other hand, however, the firm must also consider the cost of *not* training its workforce. The full potential of the IT resource could be under-exploited, leaving the firm with under-utilised, expensive equipment.

Over reliance on IT

There is a temptation to over rely on Information Technology. Information Technology cannot solve the problems faced by a business. At best, it can help to provide a possible solution, along with contributions from all the other resources of the firm.

Unfortunately, the benefits of Information Technology are widely misunderstood. It is important that a balanced view is taken of the potential performance of Information Technology, so that all the necessary additional support is put in place. For example, the data handling capabilities of computers are extensive but can only be used to full advantage if the systems for acquiring that data, whether it be by manual input or electronic transfer, are put in place.

Rapid change

There is a need to keep up with the pace of developments. The rate of change in Information Technology is rapid. The capabilities and speed of computers and processors have increased phenomenally. The problem this causes for businesses is the effort required to create and maintain a competitive advantage over competitors. Should the firm buy technology today, knowing that such equipment may be overtaken by developments within six months, or should they hold back for the next new development? If they go for the former course of action, it gives them the opportunity to steal a march on their rivals, perhaps creating a critical lead over other firms. This may create a need for extra spending in the future, as updates for the Information Technology become necessary. Once new developments are available, competitors may move ahead of the firm until it can also acquire the latest equipment or software. Investment in IT is an ongoing expense.

The financial implications

The afore mentioned points all indicate that firms must make a significant financial investment in Information Technology. Although the initial costs are very clear, the firm must be aware of the hidden costs, such as repairs and servicing and the on-going costs of updating machinery and training the workforce. So, there are significant financial costs associated with Information Technology. As with any cost, this investment must be carefully managed to prevent the costs outweighing the benefits.

PROGRESS CHECK

Discuss the possible problems of introducing Information Technology.

What is an appropriate level of investment in IT?

As with any investment, the firm must consider both the costs and the benefits to the business. A **cost:benefit analysis** attempts to quantify all the costs associated with the purchase, installation and use of Information Technology and set these against the expected benefits in terms of decreased costs, improved efficiency and higher quality output. Other financial analyses may be used to assess the risks associated with making, or not making, an investment.

Having established that a certain level of financial investment will bring a larger gain to the business, the firm also has to consider other factors which will determine whether to invest in Information Technology. These factors are discussed below.

The actions of competitors

As has been stressed throughout this chapter, Information Technology can provide a competitive advantage to a firm. The opposite perspective suggests that, as a minimum, a firm must keep pace with its competitors if it isn't to hand them such an advantage. In a competitive situation, a firm has to defend its position against the competitive actions of rivals, as well as attempting to take what advantages it can to improve its standing.

The nature of the product and market

Some products or services can be vastly improved by the introduction of Information Technology, whilst others are less suited. Banking and financial services, which for years has relied upon numerical entries on paper behind the scenes, have embraced the modern technology to the extent that any firm not providing services via Information Technology is in danger, not just of suffering competitively, but of going out of business entirely. On the other hand, services such as hairdressing have yet to find a way to harness the power of Information Technology

FACT FILE

The future is likely to bring more developments in terms of the application of IT. As well as faster computers with larger memories and new operation systems that allow machines to 'think' like humans, a survey found that amongst the most expected IT developments were:

- web TV
- virtual shopping
- intelligent materials (such as packaging that indicates when the food contents are no longer fit to be eaten)
- interactive kiosks
- voice-responsive technology
- sensors for assessing road tolls.

in a way that gives firms a significant competitive advantage. Of course, ancillary functions in such businesses, such as the keeping of financial records and stock control may benefit from Information Technology. However, the competitive strength of most firms relies on the skills of the workforce and the service provided to customers.

The culture of the business

Some businesses pride themselves on being up on the latest ideas and innovations, just as others emphasise their traditional roots. The general attitude will influence the relative importance attached to the acquisition of new Information Technology. A 'traditional' firm would have to embrace a fundamental shift in its culture and underlying ethos if it were to change its operational methods. Such a change could have a knock on effect that would change many things in the business. So, investment in IT would require the most careful consideration as it could lead to massive problems for the firm.

The size of the business

Large firms can more easily afford a large investment in Information Technology than small ones. Investment in a system of Information Technology could be a relatively large investment for a small firm. This suggests that such an investment is a greater risk for a small firm that is committing a larger percentage of its resources to the investment. If an investment in IT was to prove inappropriate, a large firm might be able to absorb the loss, whereas a small firm might find their survival threatened.

KEY POINTS

A firm is more likely to invest in IT if:

- the benefits have been demonstrated in the past
- competitors are investing
- there are clear competitive advantages.

PROGRESS CHECK

Discuss the factors which might lead to more investment in Information Technology.

Developing an IT strategy

An IT strategy is a medium to long-term plan which sets out the contribution Information Technology can bring to a firm. As with any major expenditure, there must be a careful consideration of the implications and expected gains from the project before any commitment is made.

> **Information has to be managed like any resource. This involves a clear definition of what the firm is trying to achieve with its information and an Information Technology strategy.**

The most important thing for a firm to consider when developing an IT strategy is its medium to long-term objective. If the firm wishes to become a market leader by developing a better understanding of customers and a more tailor-made response to customer needs, a large investment in Information Technology may be necessary. On the other hand, a firm attempting to penetrate new markets with existing products may place a greater emphasis on, say distribution and may give technology a lower priority. The IT strategy must help the business to achieve its goals if the investment is to be justified.

KEY POINTS

Developing an IT strategy, as with all decision-making, involves the following stages: setting objectives; gathering data; analysing data; selecting a strategy; developing a plan; implementing the plan; reviewing progress; amending or re-adopting an objective.

PROGRESS CHECK

Outline the factors which might determine a firm's Information Technology strategy

---

Summary chart

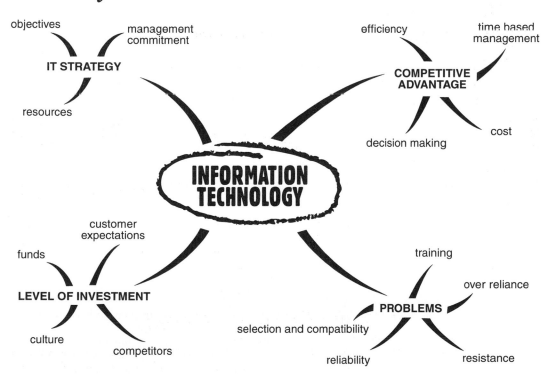

Figure 7.1 Information Technology

Approaching exam questions: Information Technology

Analyse the ways a firm might overcome employee resistance to the introduction of new Information Technology.

(9 marks)

In order to be able to answer this question appropriately, candidates must first be able to suggest some ways in which employee resistance can be overcome. They must then apply these to the question of overcoming resistance to Information Technology.

To score well on this question the candidate must demonstrate the ability to select some appropriate points, apply them to the question, and construct and develop a line of thought in a suitably analytical way. As a rough rule of thumb, consider producing one minute's writing for each mark available. It follows then that two or three separate points are all a candidate can feasibly raise.

The possible points that could be raised in this answer are:

■ the firm should employ complete openness at every step of the process

■ there should be clear communications and feedback

■ everyone should be involved at every possible stage.

Consider how a firm's objectives may influence its Information Technology strategy.

(9 marks)

As with the previous question, there are two clear parts to this question. The candidate must firstly establish the possible objectives of the firm, and then show how they might influence the Information Technology strategy.

As a point of exam style, it is a good idea to select two points that allow a degree of contrast. In this case, contrast two business objectives, one of which may lead to an expansionist approach to Information Technology, whilst the other may make the firm more cautious in adopting Information Technology.

Possible lines of thought are set out in the table below.

OBJECTIVE	EFFECT ON INFORMATION TECHNOLOGY STRATEGY
survival	minimise expenditure on anything that is risky
growth	emphasis on Information Technology that aids mass production
diversification	strive for flexibility in all aspects of Information Technology
social responsibility	consider effect on employment, community, environment etc.

Table 7.1 Possible business objectives and the likely resulting IT strategies

To what extent can Information Technology give a firm a competitive advantage in a competitive market?

(40 marks)

Any question that begins 'to what extent' is attempting to elicit a two-sided discussion and considered conclusion. One side could look at the reasons why Information Technology can give a firm a competitive advantage in these circumstances. The other side should either consider limiting factors, or other issues that can also affect competitiveness.

In this case, Information Technology can give a competitive advantage in a competitive market by:

- increasing a firm's flexibility and responsiveness to changing circumstances
- improving the quality of the products or services
- allowing the quicker development of new product ideas.

Limiting factors could include:

- the likelihood that other firms have access to the same technology
- the need for Information Technology to be integrated with all the other functions of a business.

A possible line of evaluation or conclusion could be that Information Technology is only one component involved in determining the success, or otherwise, of a business. Other factors could include the culture and status of the business, its history and reputation, the quality of production and the skills of the workforce.

'The latest Information Technology is vital to the success of any firm.' Discuss this statement.

(40 marks)

A discussion question is designed to draw a two-sided response from the candidate. A common mistake made in exams is that candidates accept the statement and construct an answer to agree with it. These statements, however, are intended to be a stimulus point for an informed discussion on a particular issue.

In this case, the question requires answers that suggest why Information Technology is a vital component of success, and which also put forward the view that the *latest* Information Technology may not be an essential part of that success.

Issues that could be raised on one hand include:

- the competitive advantage given by the latest information technology
- the flexibility it gives in responding to changing consumer demand.

On the other hand:

- Is it possible to always have the very latest advances in all aspects of Information Technology?
- Will the extra cost involved in such a strategy produce positive returns for the firm?

In conclusion, it may be said that Information Technology is likely to be one aspect of a successful firm, but not the only one and perhaps not the most important one. It is unlikely that a firm would be able to keep up to date with every small advance in Information Technology.

Student answers

Outline the possible contribution of a business culture to the successful introduction of Information Technology.

(9 marks)

Student answer

A business culture is the unwritten code to which a business operates; it is based on peoples' value and attitudes. If the culture is one that accepts change, it is more likely that Information Technology can be successfully introduced. On the other hand, a culture that values the history and traditions of the firm is likely to be resistant to change and, thus, IT may be less easy to introduce.

Marker's comments

This is a fair attempt at a balanced answer. A two-sided case is proposed and each point is dealt with, however briefly.

Mark: Content 2/2, Application 2/4, Analysis 1/3. Total = 5

How might a firm use investment appraisal techniques to determine if a potential investment in Information Technology is worthwhile?

(9 marks)

Student answer

The two main uses of investment appraisal are to assess risk and assess returns. A method such as payback is a measure of risk in that it tells a firm how long it will take for a project to recoup the initial outlay. The longer the time taken, the greater the risk that the money will not be received as circumstances change. Net Present Value, on the other hand, assesses the value of the investment, measured in present day values.

Such techniques can be used to assess whether or not the Information Technology investment is worthwhile, although the firm must be aware that these techniques are based on predictions of future events and so may not be entirely accurate. In addition, the firm ought to consider many other factors before reaching a final conclusion.

Marker's comments

This is a very full answer that adopts a clear approach to consider the issues surrounding the topic. The answer neatly broadens the discussion in the final passage to give a logical conclusion to the preceding argument.

Mark: Content 2/2, Application 4/4, Analysis 2/3. Total = 8

Evaluate the possible costs of training employees to use newly installed Information Technology.

(11 marks)

Student answer

There are many costs connected with the installation of new technology, such as training. Workers need to be made familiar with the machinery, possibly using such techniques as 'sitting with Nellie' in which one worker watches how a more experienced colleague does the job.

There are lots of costs linked to Information Technology that a firm will have to pay if it is to be successful.

Marker's Comments

This is a weak answer in which the student has attempted to link class notes on training to a more specific question. There is no attempt to assess the various different costs that the firm will face in training the workforce, and the example used is not entirely appropriate to a firm which is unlikely to have any workers experienced in using the new technology.

Mark: Content 1/2, Application and Analysis 1/6, Evaluation 0/3. Total = 2

Assess the ways in which Information Technology might provide a firm with a competitive advantage.

(11 marks)

Student answer

Information Technology can provide a firm with a competitive advantage in many ways. Two of the main ones are flexibility and quality.

The increased flexibility of the firm will allow the firm to adapt to changing situations, such as the launch of new products by competitors or the changing tastes of consumers. The firm will be more flexible as new technology is generally becoming more sophisticated, while at the same time being more generic in its application.

Effective use of Information Technology should improve decision-making.

Marker's comments

This is a fair response although it does little to develop from a promising beginning. The points have been well chosen, are generally well explained and are linked to the question. However, there is no counterpoint introduced to give a balance to the answer, such as noting that other factors are also important or that competitors may also have access to the same technology.

Mark: Content 2/2, Application & Analysis 3/6, Evaluation 0/3. Total = 5

End of section questions

1 Examine the possible impact of new Information Technology on the motivation of employees.

(9 marks)

2 Analyse the possible implications for a firm of the increasing pace of change in the development of Information Technology.

(9 marks)

3 Examine the possible influence of a business culture in determining a firm's level of investment in Information Technology.

(9 marks)

4 Consider the possible factors a firm may consider before investing in new Information Technology.

(9 marks)

5 Analyse the possible factors that may affect a firm's Information Technology strategy.

(9 marks)

6 Discuss the implications for a firm of greater investment in Information Technology.

(11 marks)

7 To what extent can Information Technology improve a firm's productive efficiency?

(11 marks)

8 Assess the possible impact leadership style may have on the successful introduction of new Information Technology.

(11 marks)

9 To what extent should a firm attempt to keep up with every advancement in Information Technology?

(11 marks)

10 Should a business be concerned if a competitor invests in more advanced Information Technology?

(11 marks)

Essays

1 Assess the possible contribution that Information Technology can make to a firm's competitiveness.

(40 marks)

2 Assess the ways in which a firm may overcome the potential problems of installing new Information Technology in its production process.

(40 marks)

3 The Chief Executive of a medium-sized engineering firm was heard to say, 'Why should I invest in new technology today, when I know it will be outdated tomorrow.' Discuss this statement.

(40 marks)

4 To what extent does a personal service firm, such as a hairdressers, rely on its Information Technology for its success?

(40 marks)

5 What proportion of a firm's resources ought to be devoted to maintaining up-to-date Information Technology?

(40 marks)

CHAPTER 8

Recent issues

Supply chain management

One of the most important recent issues in operations management is known as **supply chain management**. This involves developing and maintaining relationships with all members of the supply process; including suppliers of components, of finance and of information, as well as the distribution of these to each customer, internal or external.

Integration

The key to success in this area is **integration**: all the different elements of the supply process need to be linked together, so that each knows what the other is doing and has information on the customer's requirements to hand.

Just imagine the extremely complex processes involved in getting a can of cola onto the shelves of your local supermarket; according to the Cardiff Business School the series of activities, which starts at a mine and goes through the various smelting and rolling processes to the manufacture of the can, the printing of its label, the filling of the can with a cola drink and delivering the drink to the retailer, takes around 319 days. Making the can actually takes far longer than making the cola (and yet it is the cola which adds value) and as many as 14 warehouses are involved in this supply chain from start to finish. If this process can be simplified, better co-ordinated or made more efficient, the firms involved can make considerable savings and gain a competitive advantage.

Working with suppliers

The importance of suppliers in the production process has grown with the rise of lean production techniques and the need to be more flexible. Organisations now depend to a much greater extent on their suppliers and so finding the right ones to deal with becomes that much more important. If a firm adopts a just-in-time process, for example, this means it has no stocks to fall back on. If the supplier fails to deliver on time or the goods are faulty, production comes to a stop. A lean producer must, therefore, be able to rely totally on the supplies arriving on time and having zero defects. A supplier must be able to supply items, not only just in time but, increasingly, 'just in sequence': goods must be delivered in the same order as they are going to be used. Close collaboration with suppliers means both organisations can work together to link design, specifications and delivery. The better the

Supply chain management is the 'integration of the flow of materials, documents, information, and finance.' *(Morgan Stanley Dean Witter)*

links, the more likely it is that supplies can be delivered, fitted and used without any need for inspection or storage.

Whereas firms once tended to choose suppliers based almost exclusively on the price of their components, many are now looking at the overall costs of dealing with a particular organisation. If a suppliers' goods are more expensive but have less defects, meet the firm's own requirements more closely and can be delivered in a way which makes them easier to use without holding stocks, this may save money overall.

Good working relationships with suppliers can also speed up the development time of a new product. By working with suppliers, a firm can design products using parts which are easy to manufacture; in the past firms often designed their products in isolation and then discovered that all the components had to be designed from scratch, rather than using existing parts which had already been developed, tested and produced.

The benefits of supply chain management

The gains from better supply chain management are undeniable: estimates suggest that leading firms have managed to reduce the costs of administration, stocks, warehousing and transport from around 14% of their turnover in the late 1980s to about 7.5% in 1999. At the same time, they have reduced lead time from 27 days on average in 1987 to around 12 days in 1998. Supply chain management can also help to increase revenue – a firm which can deliver the final product more quickly than its competitors may win more orders.

> **Supply chain management can reduce costs and increase revenues.**

Managing the supply chain (i.e. all the different elements of the process from the raw materials and components, to the final delivery to the customer) has also become important because of the increasing demands of customers. Consumers are more and more interested in the source of products and the way in which they have been produced. When considering whether to buy something, increasing numbers of customers want to know where and how it was made. This means retailers have to take much more interest than they used to in the origin of the goods they sell. If, for example, a retailer like Marks and Spencer sold goods produced by a company which exploited child labour, it would lay itself open to criticism by the media. Even if the company was not directly responsible for this situation, some would argue that it could still be held accountable for the way in which its products were made. This means that leading organisations now have to look closely at all the stages of the production process, not just the stages they are directly responsible for.

The influence of Information Technology

Developments in Information Technology have helped to make supply chain management much easier than in the past – data links between retailers and manufacturers make just-in-time production more feasible, for example. At the same time, technological developments are changing the whole nature of the supply chain process. There is a decreasing need for retailers as customers deal direct with manufacturers. Companies such as Dell, which manufactures computers and sells direct, are a good example of this, and more and more firms are now developing their business on the Internet so that they can trade with their customers without the need for middlemen. This trend looks set to continue at an incredible pace. It took 35 years for the telephone to reach 100 million subscribers – it took the Internet less than two years!

> **Firms which manage their supply chain properly are more agile and leaner than their competitors.**

Interestingly, given the move towards production of items to order, the supply chain is becoming more of a 'demand chain' – firms are not producing and then hoping for demand, they are only supplying when the demand is there. The more that manufacturers move towards this model of producing to order, the less they know in advance what they will be making. To survive in these conditions and maintain their competitiveness, firms must build supply chains which are flexible and agile at every stage.

> **Demand chain thinking starts from the customer's needs and works backwards.**

Mass customisation

Customisation versus economies of scale

Consumers increasingly want more variety at a lower price. For firms this poses a fundamental problem: producing a wide range of goods is usually regarded as more expensive than producing fewer goods in larger volumes. So, if firms focus on breadth, this is likely to increase the price; if, on the other hand, they concentrate on reducing costs through economies of scale, the result may be that products are standardised and lack sufficient variety. With developments in communications and manufacturing technology, however, it is becoming easier to meet customers' desires for more choice *and* lower prices. This is because technology is offering firms the possibility of 'mass customisation'.

Designing products and processes for mass customisation

Mass customisation occurs when a firm produces products on a large scale and yet is still able to provide the customer with choice. This is achieved by developing flexible production processes and designing products which have a large number of

KEY TERM

Mass customisation
involves making basically similar products in hundreds or even thousands of variations to suit customers' specific needs.

KEY TERM

Postponement
this term refers to the customisation of the product at the end of the process. The customisation is postponed for as long as possible to enable as much as possible to be done in a standardised way. Only at the last stage are the specific needs of the customer built into the product.

parts in common. By keeping the number of different parts relatively low, an enormous amount of variety can be achieved by combining these in different ways. For example, if you develop a number of standardised elements for a personal computer (e.g memory power, software and screen size) but allow customers to decide on the combination of these, the product can be tailored to individual customer needs whilst being assembled from standardised parts.

Mass customisation allows firms to meet the needs of different market segments, to provide more personalised benefits and, at the same time, experience econmomies of scale. This has been made possible by equipment which can quickly switch from assembling the final product in one way to putting the elements together differently. Firms are now building mass customisation into their production and marketing strategies.

In the late 1990s, for example, Electrolux, the world's largest appliance group, started to develop a series of common global 'platforms' for its products which include refrigerators, vacuum cleaners and freezers. This allows the firm to develop several products built on a common framework. The result of standardising the key elements of their products has been to reduce the number of models by about 30%, whilst still offering the consumer considerable choice. Interestingly, this strategy by Electrolux came after Whirlpool, its major competitor, had tried to develop a 'world-washer', i.e. one model of washing machine designed to sell in every market. This had failed because customers reacted against too much standardisation. Electrolux sought a way of still offering variety, whilst simplifying its operations. The platform strategy is now common in several manufacturing industries, such as the car industry and consumer electronics.

MASS PRODUCTION	MASS CUSTOMISATION
stable demand	fragmented demand
large homogeneous markets	niche markets
standardised goods	customised goods
long product life cycles	short product life cycles
long product development time	short product development time

Table 8.1 Mass production and mass customisation compared (Adapted from B. Joseph Pine III *Mass Customisation*)

Enterprise Resource Planning (ERP)

As companies look for ways of improving the efficiency and effectiveness of their operations, the importance of information has increased significantly. Sharing knowledge and experience can prevent delays, encourage common problem-solving and enable solutions to difficulties to be found more quickly. As a result, there has been a rapid growth in manufacturing software programmes which enable firms to integrate their financial data, their sales data, manufacturing and stock records and their purchasing information. This is known as **Enterprise Resource Planning (ERP)**. An ERP system brings together all the relevant data to enable a company to assess how efficiently it is using all of its resources – its people, machines and money. By combining information from throughout the business, it should be easier to keep production flowing and avoid bottlenecks. Information is now seen as a vital resource which needs to be managed.

ERP overcomes the problems of 'islands of information'. This is when information is held in different parts of the organisation but is not shared throughout the firm. ERP brings together all the information needed to improve decision-making.

ERP systems and the supply chain

Software companies are now developing ERP systems that are linked to the Internet. This facilitates the sharing of information with other groups outside of the organisation, as well as being easily available to everyone within the firm. For example, customers can place orders directly on the supplier's order entry system. In the most sophisticated versions, customers can actually configure a product, work out when it will be delivered, and then go back and check the progress of the order as it is being produced. Also, suppliers can access a customer's stock levels, allowing them to replenish stocks as required. Setting up external links from a firm's ERP systems to its suppliers effectively builds an incredible, integrated supply chain in which the activities of all the different members can be clearly seen and the actions of any one member of the chain can be monitored by the others. The ultimate aim is a fully integrated supply chain in which a customer order triggers the delivery of components so that, instead of having to forecast, goods are made to order. This involves the sharing and use of information on all aspects of a firm's operations, such as its sales, lead times and stock levels, to an unprecedented degree.

The down side of ERP systems

Of course, ERP systems are not without problems. Like any computer system they can have technical faults and can be expensive to introduce. Some companies have attempted, without success, to use 'off the shelf' packages rather than tailor make systems for their precise requirements. When introducing ERP firms must ensure that staff are trained, that the system is tested and that it is adapted to the specific needs of the organisation. Whilst ERP can improve access to information which can add value for the organisation, the actual value of the system depends on how well this information is used.

Features of modern operations management

The key features of operations management in recent years have been:

- Time-based competition – the ability to produce and deliver goods more quickly than the competition

- Greater variety – the ability to meet the needs of different niche markets, and even individual customers

- Just-in-time production – the ability to produce to order

KEY TERM

An Enterprise Resource Planning system is an integrated suite of software modules that automates internal 'back office' operations for each function within an organisation, such as manufacturing, distribution, financials, purchasing, sales and human resources.
Source: *Financial Times* 15 December 1999

- Shorter product life cycles – which means that firms must be able to develop products more quickly

- Increasing emphasis on quality – which requires a clear definition of customer needs and the ability to meet these needs consistently

- Mass customisation – the ability to tailor make products to customers' requirements, whilst still benefiting as much as possible from the gains of large-scale production

- Lean production – to minimise waste

- Shorter development times – to be able to compete on time

- Total Quality Management – to involve all employees in the process of improving quality

- Delayered organisations – to speed up decision-making and to encourage the empowerment of staff

- Flexible manufacturing systems – to minimise downtime

- Greater use of IT – to improve the flow of information and enable better decision-making

- Enterprise Resource Planning – to co-ordinate information internally and externally with suppliers.

The operational challenges facing firms in the twenty-first century will be to provide the increasing levels of variety and the higher standards demanded by customers, whilst still controlling costs. The aim will continue to be to develop a nimble and lean organisation which can respond quickly and efficiently to demand. This requires a co-ordinated, responsive system in which quality and continuous improvement are built in.

The challenges of the twenty-first century also include developing (or continuing to develop) an innovative organisation. As markets change ever more rapidly, as the competition becomes ever more fierce and as customers become ever more demanding, success requires new products and new processes. Firms must build on the ideas of their workforce and create an environment in which creativity is encouraged and rewarded. Organisations must seek to change, to improve and to learn. This requires a supportive management, curious employees and an overall vision of excellence.

CHAPTER 9
Numerical data

1: Labour costs in different countries

(30 marks)

HOURLY COMPENSATION COSTS IN $US	1990	1995	1996	1997	1998
UK	12.70	13.67	14.09	15.47	16.43
France	15.49	20.01	19.93	17.99	18.28
Germany	21.88	30.83	30.26	26.90	27.20
Greece	6.76	9.17	9.59	9.20	8.91
Japan	12.80	23.82	20.91	19.37	18.05
Mexico	1.58	1.51	1.54	1.78	1.83
Sri Lanka	.35	.48	.48	.46	.47
US	14.91	17.19	17.70	18.21	18.56

Table 9.1 Pay comparisons in different countries

1 Calculate:
   a) The percentage change in labour costs in the UK from 1990 to 1998.
   b) The UK's hourly wages in 1998 as a % of those in (i) Germany and (ii) Greece

   (6 marks)

2 Analyse possible reasons for the apparent decline in hourly wage costs in France, Germany, Greece and Japan between 1996 and 1998.

   (6 marks)

3 How important do you think these figures might be in explaining the decisions of a number of US companies to relocate in South American countries such as Mexico?

   (8 marks)

4 Consider how important these figures are in determining the international competitiveness of UK companies.

   (10 marks)

2: The US steel industry

(30 marks)

THE US STEEL INDUSTRY 1998–1999	1999	1998	% CHANGE
Pig iron Production (million tonnes)	51.115	53.164	−3.9
Raw steel production (million tonnes)	107.237	108.753	−1.4
Steel imports (million tonnes)	35.731	41.520	−13.9
Imports as % of total US steel supply	21.4	26.4	
US Capacity Utilisation (%)	83.7	86.8	
Total employees (000s)	154	159	−3.1
Hourly employment costs	$35.425	$35.075	+1.0

Table 9.2 Changes in the US steel industry (Source: American Iron and Steel Institute Website)

1 Calculate total employment costs in the US steel industry in 1998 and 1999.

(3 marks)

2 Calculate capacity in the US steel industry in December 1998 and December 1999.

(3 marks)

3 To what extent does the table suggest that the US might be justified in seeking to protect its steel industry?

(6 marks)

4 Consider the possible impact of the changes in capacity utilisation identified in the table for the US steel industry.

(8 marks)

5 Discuss whether the US steel industry appears to have become more or less efficient between 1998 and 1999.

(10 marks)

3: Comparing locations

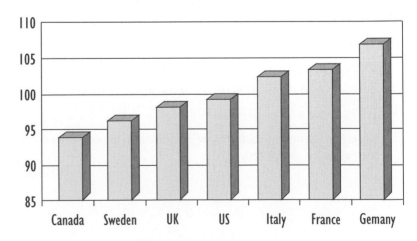

Figure 9.1 Comparison of annual total location costs by city (all countries)

Note: 100 = average cost index of US city

Source: KPMG, The Competitive Alternative, 1997

1) Calculate:
   (i) The percentage difference between locating in a Canadian city compared with one in Germany.
   (ii) The percentage difference between locating in a UK city compared with one in Sweden.

   (4 marks)

2) Analyse the factors that might explain why the location costs are so much higher in Germany than in the UK.

   (8 marks)

3) To what extent might the data in the table influence a firm's international location decision?

   (10 marks)

4) Discuss ways in which a firm's location decision might affect its profitability.

   (9 marks)

Business report 1: Harper Narrowboats

Total marks available for this question: 40

Winston Harper is a 55-year-old narrowboat builder, based on the canal at Oxford. He has specialised in narrowboats for 31 years since he left his job at a boatyard to set up in business as a sole trader, which he remains today.

He builds each boat to order as a separate job, but he has been advised by a friend who works as a management consultant that he should really be using batch production and a more mechanised approach. If Winston did this, he would make identical parts for several boats at the same time, rather than working on just one boat from start to finish.

Consider the following information, and make a recommendation to Winston as to whether he should change his production methods.

(2 marks are available for using a report format)

Appendix 1:   production details for 15 metre boat

Appendix 2:   finance figures for Harper Narrowboats

Appendix 3:   order book for last year

Appendix 4:   local competitors

Appendix 5:   past demand for narrowboats and cruisers in the Oxfordshire area

Appendix 1: Production details for 15 metre boat

	CURRENT METHODS	BATCH METHODS (ALLOWING 6 STANDARD DESIGNS)
Variable cost per boat:	£25 000	£15 000
Average stock and work in progress needed	£18 000	£38 000
Fixed capital needed	£15 000	£40 000
Order to delivery time	45 days	27 days
Additional employees needed	0	2

Appendix 2: Finance figures for Harper Narrowboats (showing existing financial position)

Price of finished boat:	£18000–£50000, depending on specification
Mark-up:	20% on full cost
Sales in 1999–2000:	7 boats
Profit in 1999–2000:	£24 000 before tax
Working Capital:	£3200
Gearing:	0%
ROCE:	192%

Appendix 3: Order book for last year

CONTRACT	MONTH COMPLETED
25 metre luxury cruiser	May
15 metre shell (No fittings)	June
18 metre basic cruiser	July
20 metre special (incl. fitted kitchen and stone fireplace)	September
20 metre shell	October
18 metre luxury cruiser	March
Conversion job on an existing 15 metre cruiser	April

Appendix 4: Local competitors

	BANBURY CRUISERS AND BARGES	HENLEY BOATS	SLAINE & TAYLOR
OUTPUT	100	135	50
Production cost of 15 metre narrowboat	£14 000	£13 500	£17 000
Mark-up	100%	110%	80%
Range	4 standard designs	6 basic designs	4 basic designs

Appendix 5: Past demand for narrowboats and cruisers in the Oxfordshire area

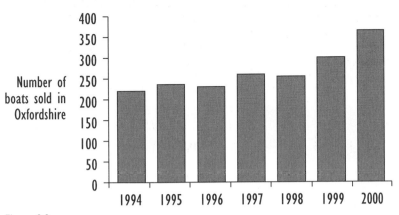

Figure 9.2

Business report 2: Shotton Ltd

Total marks available for this question: 40

J&M Shotton Ltd is a medium-sized manufacturer of light aircraft engines. Judith Shotton, the Managing Director, is considering whether or not to invest £1.5 million in a complete overhaul to update the production process. Doing so will mean calling a complete halt to production while the new equipment is installed.

Prepare a report for Judith recommending whether or not she should go ahead with the upgrade.

(2 marks are available for using report format)

Appendix 1:   critical path analysis of the upgrade

Appendix 2:   production figures

Appendix 3:   order book

Appendix 4:   productivity and cost statistics for main firms in this market

Appendix 5:   sales figures for Shotton Ltd

Appendix 6:   balance sheet, and profit and loss extracts for year to April 2000

Appendix 1: Critical path analysis of the upgrade

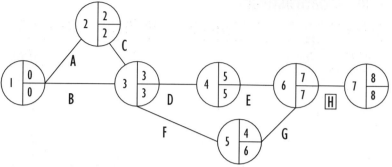

Figure 9.3

A Remove existing equipment: 2 weeks
B New equipment on order: 2 weeks
C Clean and prepare factory: 1 week
D Install new equipment: 2 weeks
E Test new equipment: 2 weeks
F Team building exercise: 1 week
G Training (external):   1 week
H Trial run: 1 week

No production will be possible during these activities.

Appendix 2: Production figures

Current capacity: 800 engines/month
Present capacity utilisation: 100%
Existing stock level: 113 engines
New capacity: 1000 engines/month
Number of employees: 20

Appendix 3: Order book

DELIVERY DATE	1 MONTH	2 MONTHS	3 MONTHS	4 MONTHS	5 MONTHS	6 MONTHS+
Orders	847	884	821	643	371	155

Appendix 4: Productivity and cost statistics for main firms in this market

COMPANY	SHOTTON	ANG (GERMANY)	JACOTTET (FRANCE)
Output per year (engines)	9600	15 700	14 900
Output per worker (engines)	48	59	61
Hourly wage cost/worker ($)	18	28	21
Capacity utilisation	100%	90%	95%
Order to delivery time	78 days	21 days	24 days
Defects/1000 engines	4.2	2.1	1.7
Price (£ at current exchange rate)	£15 000	£18 500	£17 700
Engine lifetime (flying hours)	40 000	31 000	33 000

Appendix 5: Sales figures for Shotton Ltd

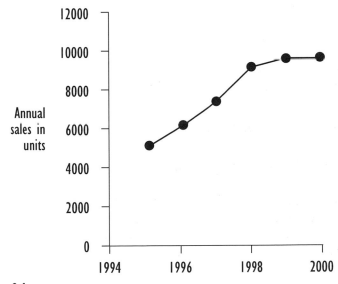

Figure 9.4

Appendix 6: Balance sheet, and profit and loss extracts for year to April 2000

Sales:	£14 400 000
Profit before tax:	£200 000
Working capital:	£(230 000)
Capital employed:	£7 020 000
Gearing:	32%

Examiner's tips

Getting to grips with operations management

There are many important issues associated with operations management and unfortunately candidates sometimes show a rather limited grasp of the underlying concepts. Perhaps most importantly, students need to appreciate how operations management contributes to the overall competitiveness of an organisation. By developing a flexible production system and offering consistently good quality, a firm can provide superior value compared to its competitors. At the same, time operations activities must complement the other functions of the organisation and fit with the firm's overall strategy. An attempt to pursue a low-cost strategy must be supported by a production system which reduces costs relative to other firms; similarly, a differentiation strategy requires a process which offers more benefits than rivals. Good candidates will try to assess an organisation's operational strengths and weaknesses and consider how these fit in terms of the opportunities and threats facing the firm.

Common mistakes

On a more basic level, students often make the following mistakes:

Confusing sales and output

Students often write answers which suggest that whatever firms produce they sell automatically. This fails to show an appreciation of demand conditions. In many cases firms produce without knowing whether or not these items will actually sell: they have to *anticipate* demand. A toy producer, for example, must estimate the Christmas demand months in advance when deciding on its production scheduling. The role of sales forecasting and the associated difficulties should be appreciated and this application should be demonstrated. If a firm ends up producing items which do not sell, its stocks increase and it incurs an opportunity cost.

Firms sell where they are based

Many answers on location show that students assume a firm's market is always the same as where it is located. In reality, a firm may sell its products all over the world. In such cases a fall in, for example, income in the local area, may have little or no effect on demand for the firm's products.

To increase profits increase output!

Very few students seem to appreciate that firms have limited capacity and this acts as a constraint on the level of output. Although the capacity can be changed over time and the scale of production increased, this may require extra finance and labour; it may also increase fixed costs. Even if demand is there, a firm cannot necessarily increase its output.

To increase profits just cut costs

When a question states that a firm is struggling, students often suggest it should cut costs; this is certainly one possible course of action open to an organisation, but candidates should consider the possible implications if this is chosen. How will costs be cut? What will this do to the quality of the product and customers' perceptions of the goods and services? Would it be better to invest more and improve the benefits on offer? Is cost cutting simply a short-term tactic which could reduce the value of the brand over the long term?

Work them harder!

Another common solution put forward by students is to work the employees harder. It is assumed that by working harder, employees can increase output quite easily. In fact, employees may not take too kindly to being asked to do more (especially if it is not in their contract or if more rewards are not on offer). Furthermore, this is not really a long-term solution – firms cannot keep pushing people harder and harder; in the long run they will need more investment or more staff! Bear in mind that the underlying problem is often to do with the way people are *managed*, or their training or equipment, rather than how hard they are working.

The importance of certain topics

Within the particular areas covered by this book, there are several specific points worth noting when preparing for exams.

Research and Development (R&D)

When writing about this topic students should always consider the objectives and the long-term success of organisations. A firm which is committed to the long-term is more likely to invest in Research and Development; a firm which focuses more on the short-term is less likely to invest. Candidates need to appreciate the importance of R&D in terms of developments in both products and processes, and at the same time appreciate why some firms take a short-term approach. The role of investors and their personal preferences is crucial here.

Students also need to consider how the level of spending on Research and Development is likely to vary from industry to industry – in sectors such as pharmaceuticals, firms make their fortunes by developing successful medicines and patenting them; they invest in R&D to develop the next product. The same is true in the music industry – firms have to be on the look out to find and develop the next band. In other industries, such as in the restaurant business, the rate of change may be slower and there may be less pressure to develop a USP (although many would argue that R&D is important whatever you do).

Lean production

Although the benefits of lean production are generally well understood by students, there is less awareness of the problems of introducing this type of production system. Employees often react badly against change (for example they may not want extra responsibility or see greater empowerment as a form of exploitation). Investors may be wary of investment in this area, especially as the benefits are likely to be long-term rather than short-term. It is important, therefore, to stress the problems a firm may face when introducing lean techniques. You also need to remember some of the difficulties which may occur even if lean production is adopted successfully throughout the organisation – problems with suppliers, employees or equipment, for example, can halt the whole production process. A good candidate will recognise the potential gains of lean production but will also acknowledge the problems of achieving and sustaining this form of production.

In particular, the need for this system to match the culture of the organisation and the importance of people within the process must be appreciated. If the culture is not appropriate, it is difficult to change it overnight.

Stocks

The main thing to remember about holding stocks is that it involves an opportunity cost. For every pile of components or semi-finished goods firms need to to consider how much money is invested in these and what else could have been done with this money. At the same time, students need to understand the reason for holding stocks and should be able to analyse the trade off between the different factors affecting the optimum level of stocks within a particular organisation. If the level of stocks is too high, it can be very expensive for the firm; if it is too low it can be very risky in terms of meeting production targets and customer demands. A strong candidate will think about the particular nature of the business in the question and highlight factors specific to its individual product; for example, fresh flowers are likely to die quite quickly, so florists must be wary of holding too much stock. Stocks of plastic flowers can be held for longer as the risk of deterioration is smaller. There is an opportunity cost, however, to holding too much stock of plastic flowers. Perhaps the florist will not be able to afford sufficient fresh stock to meet demand.

Whilst the general trend certainly is towards holding less stocks, a quick visit to your local retail store or any factory will highlight that we are a long way off true JIT production. Many firms lack the commitment, the resources, the will, the confidence, the workforce or the suppliers to try and get by with very few stocks.

Quality

The whole concept of quality is fundamentally important in business studies and yet it is often misunderstood. Far too many students still talk and write about quality in terms of expensive, top of the range items, rather than in terms of customer requirements. In many exam scripts there is some reference to improving quality;

almost inevitably this implies using more expensive materials rather than focusing on what the customer wants to a greater extent.

The way to differentiate an organisation on quality is to identify the key factors in customers' buying decisions and then consistently provide the desired benefits, time after time, at a reasonable price. High quality products require a process which prevents errors occurring; a workforce committed to improvement; a proper understanding of what customers want. The concept of quality is, therefore, firmly rooted in marketing.

Scale and productivity

Although many students are able to use the terms economies and diseconomies of scale in their answers, very few show a *precise* understanding of what they actually mean. In many cases, candidates claim that economies of scale reduce the firm's overall costs, when they actually mean unit costs. Also, few candidates get further than 'bulk buying' as an example of an economy or 'poor communication' as a diseconomy.

If you can demonstrate a fuller understanding of the different types of economy and diseconomy you will score well! Also, the *significance* of economies or diseconomies is often missed.

Wherever possible, try to put these in the context of the firm's overall strategy, its opportunities and constraints: how desirable is expansion in the first place? Does it fit with the firm's marketing strategy? Is it feasible in terms of resources? Is the demand actually there? What will be the impact on profit margins and the firm's return on capital employed? How will competitors react?

Even if economies of scale do exist, a firm may decide *not* to expand because:

■ it lacks the necessary financial resources

■ it lacks the labour required

■ it fears competitors' reactions

■ it is pursuing a niche strategy

■ the owners are happy with the present size.

The term productivity is also used rather casually in exams and is often confused with total output. Remember that productivity can be increased, even if output is not. Also remember that, even if firms do increase output, this does not guarantee a sales increase unless the demand is there.

You should also remember that attempts by managers to increase productivity are often resisted by employees who fear the impact on jobs and/or demand higher pay as a reward. Prolonged negotiations over pay and productivity are common.

The link between productivity and unit cost is an important one – after all this is why productivity matters so much to firms – and it should be developed wherever possible.

Location

It is important when studying location to appreciate its strategic importance. The right location decision can have a significant impact on a firm's costs and its revenues. For example location can mean:

■ a stronger brand image (perfume from France, whisky from Scotland)

■ access to the skilled labour (e.g. Microsoft in Cambridge in the UK)

■ an effective distribution network thanks to a good infrastructure.

A firm's location decision can influence its decision to compete on price (by enabling it to have lower costs than the competition); alternatively, location may allow a firm to charge more because it can differentiate itself in some way, perhaps by being nearer to particular scarce resources.

The location decision, therefore, affects the firm's cost structure and its revenues – a decision about where to locate should be viewed in terms of break even analysis and investment appraisal. At the same time, non-financial factors should be considered; many entrepreneurs set up in their home town just because it is their home town.

The relative importance of location for different sectors of the economy should also be considered. The three most important things in determining the success of a hotel are said to be 'location, location, location'!

On the other hand, many insurance companies could be based almost anywhere because their work is done by phone and mail, or increasingly the Internet. The growth of e-commerce means all kinds of businesses, such as banks and travel agents, have less restricted location decisions, provided they and their customers have access to the Internet.

You should also be aware of the many issues involved in relocating. Although, in general, developments in communications and transport mean firms have more freedom to choose where to locate than in the past, this does not mean that organisations can move *easily* from one location to another.

Many exam answers suggest that relocating is a relatively quick and easy decision – in reality it is usually slow and expensive. It can also be very disruptive – just think of the time it takes to let your customers and associates know you are moving. Be wary of suggesting relocation as the answer to all of a firm's problems – it rarely provides a quick fix solution.

People

Many of the topics in operations management should be considered alongside issues of Human Resource management. Flexible production can only be achieved if the people input is also flexible. The ability to respond quickly to fluctuations in demand may require temporary workers or part-time staff, for example.

Any change in production methods or working practices requires the agreement and commitment of the workforce. The importance of people in operations management is clearly highlighted in the push for Total Quality Management and lean production; these can only be successful if the workforce is committed to these changes, is willing to take responsibility for areas such as quality and believes in the importance of preventing defects from occurring.

Empowered, capable groups of employees can enable operations managers to develop processes which add real value to their organisations. A poorly trained, demotivated, badly managed workforce, on the other hand, acts as a major constraint on operations management.

So, look for opportunities to relate operations management decisions to the people in the firm. It is not just about processes.

Good luck with your exams!

Index